Repair Your Own Credit

Second Edition

By
Bob Hammond

Repair Your Own Credit

Second Edition

By
Bob Hammond

CAREER PRESS
3 Tice Road
P.O. Box 687
Franklin Lakes, NJ 07417
1-800-CAREER-1
201-848-0310 (NJ and outside U.S.)
FAX: 201-848-1727

Copyright © 1997 by Bob Hammond

REPAIR YOUR OWN CREDIT
SECOND EDITION
ISBN 1-56414-308-2, $8.99
Cover design by The Visual Group

Printed in the U.S.A. by Book-mart Press

To order this title by mail, please include price as noted above, $2.50 handling per order, and $1.50 for each book ordered. Send to: Career Press, Inc., 3 Tice Road, P.O. Box 687, Franklin Lakes, NJ 07417.

Or call toll-free 1-800-CAREER-1 (in NJ and Canada: 201-848-0310) to order using VISA or MasterCard, or for further information on books from Career Press.

Library of Congress Cataloging-in-Publication Data

Hammond, Bob.
    Repair your own credit / by Bob Hammond. — 2nd ed.
        p.   cm.
    Includes index.
    ISBN 1-56414-308-2 (pbk.)
    1. Consumer credit — United States. 2. Credit ratings — United States.   I. Title.
    HG3756.U54H367   1997   97-13338
                                                                              CIP

Acknowledgments

There are many people who helped make this book a reality. They include Ron Fry, Betsy Sheldon, Ellen Scher and Jane Brody at Career Press. Also, thanks to Anne Robinson, who assisted with revisions for the second edition.

The original edition of this book would not have been possible without the support and assistance of the following people: Peder Lund, Jon Ford, Karen Pochert, Fran Milner, Janice Vierke and Tina Mills at Paladin Press; Lona Luckett at the Better Business Bureau; Holly Novac at TRW (now Experian); Russell Deitch at the Federal Trade Commission; Gayle Weller and Susan Henrichsen with the California Attorney General's Office; Nancy Cox with the Riverside County District Attorney's Office; Elliot Blair Smith at the *Orange County Register*; Laurin Jackson at Secretarial Solutions; Lenny Robin of Fresh Start Financial Service; Dianne Huppman, Executive Director of Consumer Credit Counseling Service of the Inland Empire; Merrill Chandler of the North American Consumer Alliance; and Michael Jay, Michael Hsu, Ken Yarbrough, Greg Sullivan, Stacey Aldstadt, Carmen Vargas, June Lamond, Michael Givel, Jayson Orvis and Troy Smith. To these people, and to everyone else who made a contribution to this book—thank you.

Contents

Preface   **9**

Chapter 1
The Credit Game   **13**

Chapter 2
A Cast of Characters   **17**

Chapter 3
Your Credit Report   **25**

Chapter 4
Your Rights Under the Fair Credit Reporting Act   **33**

Chapter 5
Credit Repair: Who Needs It? What's Wrong   **41**
With It?

Chapter 6
Credit Repair Scams   **53**

Chapter 7
Questions and Answers About Credit Repair   **69**
Companies

Chapter 8
The Importance of Good Credit   **73**

Chapter 9
Seven Steps to Reestablishing your Credit   **79**

Chapter 10
Repairing Your Credit Step-by-Step   **85**

Chapter 11
The Ethics of Credit Improvement   **99**

Conclusion
Where to Get Help   **103**

Appendix   **107**

Resources   **119**

About the Author   **121**

Index   **123**

Preface

Karen Johnson had recently returned from college in Europe and had not yet established credit in the United States. One day she walked into Sam's Auto Mart and picked out a small used car with a sticker price of $12,600. She filled out a credit application, and the salesman left to process it. When the salesman returned, he told Karen he was sorry, but she did not have enough credit to qualify for the loan. Karen went to four other car dealers and got the same reaction. Slick Willie, the salesperson at Too Good Auto Sales, also told Karen that her credit history was insufficient, but added that he could help her establish new credit. Karen, frustrated and in desperate need of a car, decided to go along with Slick Willie's plan.

Slick told Karen that he had a friend who could get her a good credit rating for $900. Slick also promised to reduce the sticker price by that amount. Slick called his friend Felix Fixer and made arrangements for Karen and Felix to meet.

Karen went to Felix's office and wrote him a check for $900. She then went home to wait for Felix to call. Felix went right to work. First he called Blue Sky Bank, a subscriber to a major credit bureau. Felix convinced the clerk at the bank that he was an employee of the credit bureau and that, because of computer problems, he needed to get the bank's credit bureau access code. The clerk responded with the three-digit code.

Next, Felix searched the phone book for other people with the name of Karen Johnson. He used the access code that he obtained from Blue Sky Bank to get credit information from the credit bureau on all of the Karen Johnsons listed in the phone book. When he found a credit report for a Karen Johnson that contained only positive information, he stopped looking. He copied down all of the account information and then contacted Karen and asked her to stop by his office.

When she arrived, Felix gave her the credit information he had obtained and instructed her to use all of the information when filling out an application. He also instructed her to use a mail-drop address that he could control as her current address and to use the "victim's" Social Security number. Karen was now free to apply for credit anywhere.

Karen went back to Too Good Auto Sales and reapplied using this new information. She got the car, Slick and Felix split the $900 and Slick Willie got the commission.

This is just one example of the multitude of credit repair scams that have sprung up around the credit reporting industry, capitalizing on the credit problems of millions of American consumers and exploiting the weaknesses in the credit reporting industry. There are many more.

The flaws that exist in the credit reporting system and the abuses that have occurred in the industry have caused financial injury to a significant number of consumers. However, these flaws and abuses spawned another whole industry—credit repair—which, while perhaps well-intentioned originally, has become riddled with corruption.

Consumers should be wary of credit bureaus and credit repair services alike, because they can be burned by both. The fact is that consumers who wish to have false or inaccurate information removed from their credit reports have little need for credit clinics. Under the rules outlined in the Fair Credit Reporting Act, they can do it themselves easily and inexpensively.

Repair Your Own Credit was written for those consumers who have had credit problems and are considering the services of a credit repair company. It is meant to warn consumers of the dangers and pitfalls of credit repair and to empower them to help themselves. The book is a result of many years of research into the subject of consumer credit, including my own personal experiences as a credit consultant and consumer activist. It is based on firsthand accounts of some of the major players in the credit game.

Repair Your Own Credit takes a revealing, if not shocking, look at the scams and scoundrels that gave the credit repair business such a bad reputation and tells how they ended up. Many of my former associates have cautioned that I may be sacrificing my own livelihood and perhaps even my own freedom and safety by publicizing this book, and perhaps that is so. But to paraphrase Benjamin Franklin, "Those who would give up essential publicity to purchase a little security deserve neither."

Chapter 1

The Credit Game

••

For many years, I was engaged in research—studying various strategies for attaining the personal and financial freedom that comes with debt-free wealth. I spent thousands of dollars on books, tapes, newsletters and home-study courses. I attended countless seminars and consulted with numerous self-proclaimed experts on real estate, creative financing, positive thinking, multilevel marketing, mail-order publishing and other plans. Some were very valuable and informative. Others were total ripoffs. I also came across several underground books that claimed to reveal inside secrets and strategies for beating the system. Some of these books contained very interesting and useful information. Others turned out to be not only completely illegal, but frightening as well.

I finally began to get discouraged. None of these plans lived up to their promises. The only ones who seemed to be getting rich were the promoters themselves. I was tired of being ripped off. I still couldn't help thinking, however, that there must be a way for someone like myself, with an average education and abilities, to get ahead in the world.

One day I attended a seminar in Riverside, Calif., led by an authority on consumer credit. The seminar also featured a former credit bureau executive turned consumer advocate. I listened intently as they took turns explaining credit bureau operations, consumer rights under the Fair Credit Reporting Act (FCRA), how to have negative information removed from credit files and the secrets of establishing a new credit identity. The final hour of the seminar was devoted to instructions on setting up a profitable credit consulting firm. I was intrigued by the possibilities. Somehow, this one seemed a little different than the others. Little did I know that it was about to become a major turning point in my life. I left the seminar with an entirely new understanding of the phrase "knowledge is power."

Eagerly, I began the process of clearing up the wreckage of my past and getting my own house in order. My own credit had been devastated by bankruptcy, divorce and many years of reckless living. I was amazed to discover that, by applying what I had learned at the seminar, in a matter of weeks, companies that had rejected me previously were suddenly begging me to take their credit cards. I wanted to shout it from the rooftops— "It works! It really works!"

For several years I worked as a credit consultant with my own company. In working with others, I discovered that *most* people had information in their credit files that was obsolete, inaccurate or misleading. In many cases, the information belonged to someone else with a similar name. I discovered that people were being discriminated against and turned down for credit, insurance, jobs and even places to live because of the clerical error of some bureaucrat.

During this time I was involved in a lawsuit against TRW Information Services (now called Experian), one of the largest and most powerful of the consumer credit reporting services or credit bureaus. That prompted me to do some additional research into the way credit bureaus violated the rights of citizens.

The culmination of this research was the publication of *How to Beat the Credit Bureaus: The Insider's Guide to Consumer Credit*. This book showed how the credit bureaus were violating the Fair Credit Reporting Act, and it presented case studies of people who had taken legal action against the bureaus on grounds of defamation, invasion of privacy and negligence.

Consequently, hundreds of lawsuits were filed against the major credit bureaus throughout the country. TRW was among them, with the Federal Trade Commission (FTC) and 19 states filing lawsuits against it. The credit bureaus were forced to make it easier for consumers to obtain information regarding their files and also to dispute erroneous information. TRW and Equifax awarded thousands of dollars in damages to consumers and agreed to major concessions and policy changes.

Meanwhile, with 70 percent of American consumers as potential clients, the credit repair industry developed quickly to meet the needs of the millions of individuals with poor credit ratings. Along the way, a parade of con artists and self-proclaimed credit gurus took advantage of an opportunity, leaving behind a wake of bare-pocketed consumers. In recent years, American consumers have lost more than $50 million collectively by hiring fly-by-night operators to "fix" their credit reports—with few or no results. Thousands of consumers have complained of being ripped off by unscrupulous promoters of credit repair scams. New federal legislation was passed in an attempt to put a stop to these companies and their deceptive practices.

The following pages provide a shocking inside look at the scams used by credit clinics to bilk millions of dollars from gullible consumers on a daily basis. They also explain how you can work to repair your own credit, for little or no money.

Chapter 2

A Cast of Characters

•••

There are many types of players in the consumer credit game: creditors, credit reporting bureaus, credit repair agencies, the Federal Trade Commission, Congress and state authorities, not to mention lobbyists at both the state and federal levels. All of them are in the game to make money or protect a means of making it, or to regulate the industry, but none of these players are truly here for you—the individual consumer of credit. Every person who uses credit (which is more than 90 percent of all American adults) should become familiar with the agencies that influence their credit reputations. Knowledge is the first and best avenue to power the individual consumer can have. A brief introduction to the major characters follows, and you will find expanded information in the chapters that follow.

Creditors

For the purposes of this discussion, a creditor is any company, organization or institution that permits you to use future income to purchase goods and services today. A creditor could be the issuer of a credit card, the company that holds your mortgage or the bank that helped finance your auto loan. In exchange for advancing you credit to purchase goods or services, creditors expect repayment with interest. Creditors have a keen interest in your payment habits: Will you pay on time? Will you pay the full amount? What have other creditors experienced with you in the past? Many creditors rely on another major player in the credit game, the credit reporting service, to provide them with information about your credit history.

Credit reporting services

There are more than 1,200 credit reporting services in the United States, but there are three in particular that every credit consumer should get to know: Experian, Equifax and Trans Union. These are national/international agencies that collect credit history information on hundreds of millions of American consumers. This information is provided to them by individual creditors such as department stores, mortgage companies and banks, known as *subscribers* in credit bureau parlance. (Public information, including bankruptcy filings and other legal actions, is also collected by the credit reporting bureaus.) Creditors then purchase complete credit histories on individual consumers from the bureaus. These credit histories are used to evaluate a consumer's creditworthiness when considering extension of credit. Other agencies or individuals may purchase credit information as well, including employers and insurance and law enforcement agencies.

The three major credit bureaus each have affiliate bureaus that collect credit history information on a more regional basis. These regional agencies enter into a relationship with one of the big three bureaus, with the regional agency storing its information on the national bureau's database. There are also mortgage reporting agencies, which are localized agencies that serve the real estate market, and provide credit reports that are a composite of information available through the major credit bureaus.

Experian

Experian, formerly TRW Inc., is based in Orange, Calif. It is one of the nation's largest computerized consumer credit reporting services, maintaining credit information on more than 180 million consumers in the United States. Experian collects and stores that information and provides it to subscribers that have a "permissible purpose" to use it as defined by the Fair Credit Reporting Act (FCRA). Permissible purposes include granting credit, hiring for employment and underwriting insurance policies. Organizations and companies that subscribe to Experian's service include credit grantors, employers and insurance underwriters.

Experian entered the credit reporting business when, as TRW, it acquired Credit Data Corporation in 1969. This bureau, originally the Detroit-based Michigan Merchants Credit Association, was founded in 1932. At the beginning of the 1960s, the company used file cabinets and 3-by-5-inch cards to store consumer credit information. In 1965, Credit Data initiated and installed the first computerized, on-line credit reporting system. For more than two decades, TRW was the technological leader in the credit reporting industry. It was the first to automate its nationwide database to ensure that consumers' credit histories were kept when they moved or changed their names.

In early 1996, TRW sold its $1.1 billion information businesses to investors led by Bain Capital Inc. and the Thomas H. Lee Co. The company changed its name to Experian. In November 1996, Great Universal Stores PLC purchased Experian and merged it with the CCN Group of Nottingham, United Kingdom, creating a global information leader that is first or second in every market it serves, including the United States, Japan, Australia, France, Germany, the United Kingdom and more. Experian retains the technological edge it held for so long as TRW; it recently launched FileOne™, a new consumer credit data management system that is the world's largest commercial relational database.

In return for the credit information and services offered by Experian, subscribers provide Experian with a record of their past and present credit account information, usually on a monthly basis. This regular receipt of credit information provides Experian with an automatic update of consumer credit account information.

The subscribers' information is typically copied directly from the billing records used to notify customers. Information is sent to Experian's data center in Allen, Texas, where it undergoes a data-verification process before being entered into the company's computer system. Public record information, including bankruptcy filings, is gathered directly from court and county records, converted to a computerized format and entered into the computer system.

Experian's search and retrieval system can check all areas of the country with a single inquiry. Any previous addresses, alternate surnames such as maiden names and nicknames can be retrieved automatically with the current consumer information.

Trans Union

Trans Union, based in Chicago, Ill., is another primary source of credit information, serving a range of industries that routinely evaluate credit risk or verify information about customers. The company's consumer credit information file includes public records information and accounts receivable information from national, regional and local credit grantors. Trans Union claims their database includes credit activity information on every credit-active person in the United States.

Equifax

Equifax, based in Atlanta, Ga., operates the largest credit reporting network in the U.S., including company-owned and affiliated credit bureaus; its annual revenues top $1.6 billion. As with Experian and Trans Union, Equifax offers a variety of information services, but reporting of credit information is its primary business. Its customers include the nation's largest retailers, banks and financial institutions, as well as utilities, automobile dealers and rental companies, credit unions, hotels and motels and others. Its international operations include divisions in Canada, Europe and South America.

Associated Credit Bureaus

Associated Credit Bureaus (ACB) is a trade association, headquartered in Washington, D.C., with more than 1,450 credit reporting, collection service and mortgage company members. Its primary functions are legislative affairs, industry operating standards, public relations and education. ACB serves as a spokesperson for the credit reporting industry with the media, and sets voluntary industry standards in addition to providing "legislative support" (lobbying) at the federal and state level. ACB has been very effective in influencing the amendment of federal law to meet its "industry standards" and preventing adoption of measures favored by consumer advocates that would have limited the amount consumers can be charged to receive copies of their own credit reports.

Credit repair agencies

Credit repair agencies, "credit clinics" or "credit doctors" as they are often called, are companies that claim to be able to influence your credit rating—to change it for the better. They will often claim to have the ability to have negative items removed from your credit by taking advantage of "little-known loopholes in the law." To perform this service they charge a fee, ranging from $100 to $2,000 or more. Historically, such "businesses" have often been scam operations, skipping town before unwary customers realize their credit ratings are unchanged but their bank balance has dropped. Although some of these businesses are legitimate, no credit repair agency can do any more to affect your report than you can yourself, and no credit agency can remove negative information from your credit report if it is correct. Unfortunately, current conditions in the credit market indicate many consumers are easy targets for such scams, with more than 70 million consumers having substantially negative credit ratings. In Chapter 6 I'll explain many of the tactics such agencies use, many of which are illegal, and in Chapter 10 you'll learn how you can repair your own credit.

The Better Business Bureau

The Better Business Bureau (BBB) was originally founded by Samuel C. Dobbs in 1906 as a vigilance committee to combat unfair advertising practices. While truth in advertising remains a primary concern for the more than 150 Better Business Bureaus that exist across the country, their mission has expanded to include other programs and goals to make the marketplace a fair and honest place to do business.

The BBB considers the credit repair industry to be one of the most problematic in recent years. Many players in the industry have taken advantage of the poor credit ratings that plague so many consumers. Although there may be legitimate organizations that can help an individual improve or correct credit histories, the industry in general suffers from a well-earned reputation of being a scam. The reason? Unfair and deceptive claims that bad credit can be "erased," or "made extinct." These misrepresentations of services—in advertising and sales pitches—have prompted the Better Business Bureau to wage war on these scam artists through cooperation with law enforcement investigations, advertising challenges, reliability reports to the public, media proposals and, most importantly, consumer education.

The National Foundation for Consumer Credit

The National Foundation for Consumer Credit is a nonprofit membership organization whose goals are to educate, counsel and promote the intelligent use of credit in individual and family financial planning. As the national organization, NFCC provides leadership for a growing number—now almost 1,000—of nonprofit community Consumer Credit Counseling Services in the United States and Canada.

Consumer Credit Counseling Services

Consumer Credit Counseling Service (CCCS) is the nation's largest nonprofit organization providing confidential and professional financial and debt counseling to aid and rehabilitate financially distressed customers with debt problems due to job loss, reduced income, divorce, catastrophic illness or poor financial management. Annually, more than one million people seek the assistance of CCCS, and many of them approach the organization as a last resort to bankruptcy. It is important to note that CCCS, though a nonprofit agency, is largely funded by 10,000 creditors, 31 percent of whom are credit-card issuers. Though CCCS has been beneficial to millions of consumers with credit problems, it also answers to the creditors, and rarely recommends bankruptcy, although the conditions may be quite legitimate.

Debt Counselors of America

Debt Counselors of America is another nonprofit organization that assists families and individuals with debt, credit, money and financial questions, problems or difficulties. The services they provide are confidential, and are free or available at a low cost. The programs they offer include ONE-PAY, in which many creditors will reduce or eliminate interest, stop late charges, bring past due accounts current and stop collection calls. Debt Counselors of America has taken a high-tech approach, utilizing Internet technology to provide clients with 24-hour access to their accounts on their secure website. The Web Account Access System shows the latest amount, date and transaction number posted for each individual creditor owed, so that clients can monitor and review the progress they are making in repayment of debt.

Chapter 3

Your Credit Report

• •

Across the United States there are several thousand credit bureaus collecting credit information about consumers. These credit bureaus are connected to centralized computer files that contain data on millions of individuals. Almost instantaneously, a credit bureau can produce for a subscribing creditor a revealing report about your past and present credit activity.

Although they can operate in different ways, many bureaus follow similar procedures. Banks, finance companies, merchants, credit card companies and other creditors are the paying customers (subscribers) of credit bureaus. Subscribers regularly send credit reports on their customers to the credit bureaus, which contain information about the kind of credit extended, the amount and terms, and the paying habits of individual customers. Some information is collected by the credit bureaus from other sources, such as court records.

What your file may contain

The credit bureau file contains your name, address, Social Security number and birth date. A lot of other information also may be included:

- Your employer, position and income.
- Your former address.

- Your former employer.

- Your spouse's name, Social Security number, employer and income.

- An indication that you own your home, rent or board.

And your file probably contains detailed credit information. Each time you buy on credit from a reporting store or take out a loan at a bank, finance company or other reporting creditor, a credit bureau is informed of your account number, the date, amount, terms and type of credit.

As you make payments, your file is updated to show the outstanding balance, the number of payments and amounts past due, and the frequency of 30-, 60- or 90-day lateness. The file also contains public record information about you, including any tax liens, wage garnishments or legal judgments. Previous late payments, collection actions and legal judgments can cause a lender to reject your credit application, or it can result in higher interest rates and extra finance charges (known as "points") that can make a difference of hundreds or thousands of dollars on a major purchase, such as a car or home. Your record may also indicate the largest amount of credit you have had and the maximum limit permitted by the creditor.

Each time a potential credit grantor reviews your report, it is called an *inquiry*, and it is recorded as part of the report. The number of inquires on your report can be influential to a potential credit grantor. If there are numerous inquiries without credit having been subsequently extended, then the creditor may conclude that you have been turned down. More and more often, numerous inquiries are considered ominous by potential creditors, regardless of the outcome.

Requesting your credit report

Copy and use the "Credit Report Request" letter (shown in Chapter 10) to request a copy of your credit report from the major credit reporting agencies listed in this section. Be sure to enclose a copy of your driver's license, credit card bill or utility bill. If you have been denied credit within the past 60 days, you can, by law, receive a free report from the agency that provided the report. Your request must be accompanied by a copy of the denial letter. At one time, Experian (formerly TRW Inc.) offered consumers one free copy each year regardless of whether or not they had been turned down for credit. This policy ended in 1996.

Note: Each agency may not have the same information, so you may want to obtain a copy of your report from all of them. As of October 1, 1997, the Fair Credit Reporting Act (FCRA) stipulates that cost to consumers for copies of their credit reports is $8, adjusted annually for inflation, unless otherwise regulated by state law. A few states have lower amounts. And remember, if you have been denied credit, you may request the report at no charge within 60 days.

Experian
P.O. Box 949
Allen, TX 75013
800-682-7654

Equifax Credit Information Services
P.O. Box 740241
Atlanta, GA 30374-0241
800-685-1111

Trans Union Credit Information
Trans Union Consumer Relations
760 West Sproul Road
P.O. Box 390
Springfield, PA 19064-0390
800-851-2674

What the credit report says

Credit reports include basic information about consumers, including name, address, Social Security number, marital status, date of birth, spouse's name, number of dependents, previous addresses and employment information. This is followed by a listing of credit information that includes credit account numbers, the creditor's name, the amount of last payment, the credit limit of the account and the timeliness of credit payments. Some reports contain a listing of public information, including tax liens, court judgments and bankruptcies. Last, there is an inquiry section that notes creditors who have reviewed a copy of the credit report. This section serves as an audit trail for consumers, to ensure that no unauthorized parties have accessed the report.

Unfortunately, if you're like 70 percent of American consumers, you probably have at least one item in your credit report that is negative. Trouble is, the information may well be incorrect, misleading, inaccurate or obsolete. Your file could contain information about someone else with a similar name or Social Security number. (The industry term for this is "commingling" of files, and it is a common problem.) Much of the public record information is gathered manually, increasing the odds that it is reported incorrectly in your file.

I recommend that everyone review their credit report annually, regardless of your credit and debt status. Associated Credit Bureaus estimates that *two billion* pieces of information about consumer trade activity are entered into consumer credit records each month—with that incredible volume, mistakes are sure to happen, and it's in your best interest to catch and correct them before they become a stumbling block in obtaining credit.

Positive, neutral and negative notations

The information in your report is usually divided into three types of ratings: positive, neutral and negative. The following are the only statements in your credit report that are considered positive:

1. Paid satisfactorily or paid as agreed.

2. Current account with no late payments.

3. Account/credit line closed at consumer's request.

The following notations are considered neutral, but in reality, anything less than a positive rating is considered negative by many credit grantors.

1. Paid, was 30 days late.

2. Current, was 30 days late.

3. Inquiry.

4. Credit card lost.

5. Refinance.

6. Settled.

7. Paid.

The following are considered negative:

1. Bankruptcy—Chapter 7 or Chapter 13.

2. Judgments.

3. Liens.

4. Account closed—grantor's request.

5. Paid, was 60, 90 or 120 days late.

6. SCNL (subscriber cannot locate).

7. Paid, collection.

8. Paid, charge-off.

9. Bk liq reo (bankruptcy liquidation).

10. Charge-off.

11. Collection account.

12. Delinquent.

13. Current, was 60, 90 or 120 days late.

14. CHECKPOINT, TRANS ALERT or CAUTION (potential fraud indicators).

15. Excessive inquiries (looks as if you've been turned down by everyone else.)

What is credit scoring?

In addition to the analysis of the credit report, many creditors use a system called credit scoring to determine whether you're a good credit risk. The creditor uses a system that measures a variety of personal financial factors, and it awards points based on the importance the creditor assigns to each factor. Among the factors considered are income, credit payment history, whether or not you own a home and the number of years you have held your job. Creditors generally offer credit to consumers awarded the most points, because these are assumed to predict who is likely to pay back debt.

To illustrate how credit scoring works, consider the following example which uses only three factors to determine whether or not someone is creditworthy. (Most systems use six to 15 factors, and some go as high as 20.)

Example:

Monthly Income	Points awarded
Less than $400	0
$400-$650	3
$651-$800	7
$801-$1,200	12
$1,200+	15

Age	Points awarded
21-28	11
28-35	5
36-48	2
48-61	12
61+	15

Telephone in home	Points awarded
Yes	12
No	0

If, for example, a score of 25 was necessary to receive credit, you would need enough income at a certain age (and perhaps a telephone) to qualify. Remember, this system illustrates very generally how a credit scoring system works; most systems review many more factors. Credit scoring systems, if properly constructed , allow creditors to evaluate customers consistently and impartially. Many creditors design their systems so that marginal casesñthose that are not high enough to pass easily or low enough to fail definitely—are assigned to a credit manager who reviews the information and makes the decision.

But one major drawback to this system is that credit scoring is becoming increasingly popular, and the major credit bureaus—Experian, Equifax and Trans Union—are also in the business of evaluating your file information, assigning a credit score (or "risk score," as it is also known), and providing that information to subscribers for a fee.

Increasingly, the decision of whether or not to extend credit to a consumer is being done by computers, and credit scores enter into this mechanized evaluation. While the Fair Credit Reporting Act (FCRA) requires credit bureaus to show you what is in your file and requires bureaus to correct inaccurate information, the Federal Trade Commission has recently determined that credit bureaus do not have to disclose "risk scores" to consumers who request copies of their reports. This judgment was made based on the notion that the "risk score" is not actually in the credit bureau's files on a consumer, and therefore the FCRA does not require that it be disclosed. (For more specifics, see Chapter 4.)

This unfortunate turn of events leaves consumers with the ability to challenge information in their credit report that may influence the credit score, but they don't have the legal tools to know the score itself or to challenge the score, even if it is the reason they are denied credit.

Your Rights Under the Fair Credit Reporting Act

• •

For more than 25 years, the Fair Credit Reporting Act (FCRA) has been a primary tool consumers have had available to protect themselves against abuses of the credit reporting system. Congress passed the FCRA in 1971 to regulate the use of credit reports, to require credit bureaus to delete obsolete information and to give the consumer access to his or her file and the right to have erroneous data corrected. It also placed important limits on the types of persons, businesses and organizations that can access this very personal information about consumers.

In late 1996, Congress passed legislation updating the law, with most provisions taking effect October 1, 1997. This chapter summarizes your basic rights under the law, noting those changes that are part of the 1996 update. It's important to familiarize yourself with the law because mistakes do occur in the credit reporting industry, and such mistakes can affect, sometimes drastically, the lives and livelihoods of responsible citizens.

Limitations on access to information

The FCRA stipulates that a credit report about you may be issued only to properly identified persons for approved purposes. It may be furnished in response to a court order or in accordance with your own written request; and it may be provided to someone who will use it in connection with evaluation of a credit transaction, employment, underwriting of insurance, determination of eligibility for a license or other benefit granted by a governmental agency or other legitimate business need. Your friends and neighbors who are curious about your affairs may not obtain information about you. To do so might subject the subscriber who obtained it for them to fine and/or imprisonment.

You, too, may review your file

The FCRA gives you the right to know what your credit file contains, and the credit bureau must provide someone to help you interpret the data. You will be required to identify yourself to the bureau's satisfaction, and you will be charged a fee. There is no fee, however, if you have been turned down for credit, employment or insurance because of information contained in a report within the preceding 60 days. The credit bureau that reported the adverse information about you is required, by law, to provide you with a copy of your report free of charge. Otherwise the fee is typically $8, unless otherwise stipulated by state law (a few states mandate lower fees).

The 1996 update to the FCRA expanded the right to receive a free credit report to include the following: unemployed persons who plan to apply for a job within 60 days; persons receiving public assistance (welfare); persons who have been notified by a collection agency affiliated with a credit bureau that a collection action is about to be reported to the bureau; and victims of credit fraud.

Time limits on adverse data

The FCRA states that negative credit history items may only be reported for seven years, which covers most items that would be reported. A significant exception is a declaration of personal bankruptcy—a fact may be reported for 10 years. (The FCRA does not limit how long positive information can be reported.) After seven years or 10 years, the information can no longer be disclosed by a credit reporting agency, with a few exceptions; (1) if you are submitting a credit application for $150,000 or more; (2) if you are seeking to purchase life insurance of $150,000 or more; or (3) if you are applying for employment at an annual salary of $75,000 or more. In these situations the time limits on releasing negative data do not apply.

The amounts cited here are effective October 1, 1997. Prior to that date, the limits were $50,000 on credit or life insurance applications, and $20,000 on employment applications. In addition, the 1996 FCRA update requires that any employer or prospective employer who wishes to pull your credit report (after October 1, 1997) must have your *written permission* to do so, and the request cannot be hidden in small type in an employment application—it must be signed separately. If you are rejected for a job based "in whole or in part" on an item in the credit report, the employer must give you a copy of the report *before* turning you down, and it must give you written instructions on how to challenge the accuracy of the report.

As of this writing, it remains to be seen if the new restrictions on employers will be effective, but it appears the consumer/job applicant will have a hard time realizing benefits to privacy protection. For instance, what is the prospective employer's responsibility to continue consideration of a job candidate if he or she refuses to permission to have their credit file accessed? Even if a company does reject an prospective employee based on adverse information in a credit report, what stops the company from claiming a different reason for turning the applicant down? Obviously, it can literally pay to know what's in your credit report! The 1996 FCRA update does provide, however, that credit bureaus must show the name or full trade name of anyone that has requested your credit report in the past year, and for employers, the past two years.

Incorrect information

Credit bureaus are required to follow reasonable procedures to ensure that subscribing creditors report information accurately. However, mistakes often occur. Your file may contain erroneous data or records of someone with a name or Social Security number similar to yours. When you notify the credit bureau that you dispute the accuracy of information, the bureau is required to reinvestigate within 30 days and, if necessary, modify or remove inaccurate data. Any pertinent information you have concerning an error should be given to the credit bureau. The bureau may not charge you for this reinvestigation. Within five business days of completing the investigation, results must be sent to the consumer, along with a copy of the credit report. The new law also requires that corrected information must be shared among the major credit bureaus.

The credit bureau turns to the reporting agency (the creditor) to verify disputed information. If the information cannot be verified within the 30-day time limit, it must be deleted. The 1996 FCRA update stipulates that if the creditor verifies the information at a later date, negative information can be reinserted to the file, and the credit bureau must notify the consumer. A creditor cannot provide information they know or consciously avoid knowing is incorrect. If they have made a mistake, they are required to notify all major credit bureaus to which they have reported the incorrect information.

Adding your own statement to the file

If reinvestigation does not resolve the dispute to your satisfaction, you may enter a statement of 100 words or less in your file, explaining why you think the record is inaccurate. The law, however, *does not* require a credit bureau to add to your credit file a statement of circumstances that explains a period of delinquency caused by some unexpected hardship, such as serious illness, a catastrophe or unemployment, which eliminated or drastically reduced your income. This type of explanation should be given by you directly to a credit grantor when applying for credit.

The credit bureau is required to include your statement about disputed data—or a coded version of it—with any reports it issues about you. At *your request*, the bureau must also send a correction to anyone who received a report in the preceding six months if it was for a credit check, or within a two-year period if it was for employment purposes. Under the 1996 FCRA update, you can be charged for this, but no more than the creditor would be charged to receive the information.

High-tech credit relief

In addition to new legislation, technological advances have made it easier and faster for consumers to fight credit-report errors and update their report. Until recently, consumers who disputed, say, an entry about a credit card account have had to send separate letters to the three national credit bureaus— Equifax, Trans Union and Experian. The bureaus, in turn, would ask the creditor that supplied the questionable data to verify the items, which could take 30 days or more. Now credit bureaus and creditors use the Automated Consumer Dispute Verifaction (ACDV) system that automatically reports errors to all the major bureaus. Previously, credit bureaus and creditors mailed paper copies of such data to one another.

The ACDV system was adopted voluntarily by the three major credit bureaus and major creditors, and it appears it will be the mechanism used to comply with the new requirement that changes in reported information must be automatically shared by the bureaus.

The special status of credit scoring

Although much has been done to regulate credit reports, other products and services provided by credit bureaus (which are information-gathering agencies) are subject to different, fewer or no regulations. Credit scoring is a service the major bureaus provide to a variety of clients, rating the creditworthiness of individuals based on their credit histories and other types of personal information that may be available. These scores are increasingly being used by creditors to determine whether or not a specific consumer is a good credit risk. In fact, Fannie Mae and Freddie Mac (formerly federal agencies with significant influence over lending policies) determined that all applications for mortgages with federal connections must be evaluated using credit scoring by late 1996.

The scores provided by the bureaus are based, at least in part, on the information contained in the credit report (which, as we know, can be wrong). Consumer groups have advocated that the bureaus be required to share the credit score with the consumer. The Federal Trade Commission (FTC), which is charged with enforcing the FCRA, issued a ruling on this question on September 1, 1995. It said, in part:

> *The Federal Trade Commission said today that federal law does not require credit bureaus to disclose "risk scores" to consumers who request copies of their credit reports. The FTC reminded consumers, however, that they are still entitled to see their credit reports and to learn from creditors what in their reports led to their denial of credit, if that happens. Today's Commission action follows review of more than 300 pages*

of public filings in response to the FTC's request of last summer for comments on its 1992 interpretation of the Fair Credit Reporting ACT (FCRA), in which the FTC said the FCRA did require disclosure of "risk scores"....

The FCRA, which is enforced by the FTC, gives consumers the right to obtain the nature and substance of all information (except medical information) that is in a credit bureau's files on them at the time they make a request for such information. Because "risk scores" are not in the consumer's file, the FTC concluded the FCRA did not require disclosure.

Consumer advocates consider this ruling to be a classic case of the tail wagging the watchdog. Though the FTC originally announced it would require disclosure of "risk scores", the credit bureaus succeeded in having the ruling reversed, claiming substantial costs would be associated with providing "risk scores" and asserting that consumers were likely to be confused by the scores rather than benefit from knowing them. The bureaus noted the FCRA requires a credit bureau to disclose only the "nature and substance of all information...in its files on the consumer at the time of the request" for disclosure by the consumer, but it does not require them to reveal a statistical assessment such as a "risk score" that is not contained in the file.

Chapter 5

Credit Repair: Who Needs It? What's Wrong With It?

● ●

Who needs credit repair? If you're like 70 percent of credit-using consumers, the answer could well be you. You may have encountered past financial difficulties that affect your ability to use credit today. At some point in your life, you may develop a negative credit history you need to overcome. Or you may be among the many unfortunate consumers with incorrect and negative information on your report. Although the credit reporting industry purports to be concerned with accuracy of information, errors are not exactly uncommon, and trying to fix them can be an ordeal.

For instance, a Santa Ana, Calif., woman wrote letters and made telephone calls to the major bureaus for six months trying to get another person's bad credit history out of her file. A Chicago man with the same problem couldn't convince a credit bureau there was a mistake, even though the age and addresses of the similarly named man whose information appeared on his report were obviously different from his. A suburban St. Louis, Mo., couple had a bankruptcy filing mistakenly placed in their file. Banks shut off loans to their struggling construction business, forcing them to file bankruptcy for real. They sued, but lost.

Then there's the case of a Los Angeles woman whose credit was destroyed when someone used her Social Security number to open 15 fraudulent charge accounts and charged nearly $15,000 worth of merchandise. The woman challenged the credit bureau reports and informed them that information supplied on the credit applications—including name, birth date, and employment—was incorrect, but the credit bureau did little to investigate her claim. She endured a two-and-half year credit nightmare, and in 1996, a federal jury awarded her $200,000 in damages when she sued Trans Union. She settled with Equifax and TRW (now Experian). The jury found that Trans Union had not conducted a investigation of her complaint or followed reasonable procedures to assure accuracy. It is required to do both by the Fair Credit Reporting Act (FCRA).

The credit bureau mentality

In their well-intentioned efforts to protect the integrity of the information they report, the major credit reporting bureaus have developed a mind-set that, at times, seems determined to block, squelch and otherwise frustrate consumers who are affected by the information they sell.

The bureaus try to report the truth about consumers and their spending/payment habits—an occupation that has its ugly side. Certainly there are deadbeats who want to fraudulently change accurate and negative information in their reports. But at times the bureaus are so vigilant in protecting reported information, it seems they are determined to prevent consumers from taking action to protect themselves and their credit reputations. Strategies for this include interpreting the FCRA in ways that support credit bureau inaction (hiding behind the law) and training subscribers to interpret neutral data in a negative way (too many inquiries make consumers a poor credit risk).

Industry secrecy

In determining whether to grant or deny credit, credit grantors use the five "Cs": character, capacity, capital, collateral and conditions. The major credit bureaus have developed an elaborate system by which to identify the "character" of a consumer. The system looks at the individual's credit report and, more specifically, his or her bill-paying habits.

Trade secrets and proprietary information are safeguarded and released only to those who have a "need" to know. For that reason, it is nearly impossible to find one individual within a credit bureau who is aware of all aspects of credit reporting. Credit bureaus have compartmentalized each of their operational and marketing functions so that individual employees know only one small aspect of the business.

Moreover, specific structures of power and influence within each department further promote this environment of secrecy. The public affairs and legislative affairs departments are used to convey information to the public and legislative and enforcement bodies. No matter how well-intentioned the managers of either of these departments may be, they simply parrot information that has been carefully guided through the corporate political maze.

Taking cover under the law

Congress enacted the Fair Credit Reporting Act as a means of protecting consumer rights. It was not intended to give specific authority for credit bureaus to operate a profit-making enterprise. However, the FCRA is precisely what credit bureaus quote most often in an attempt to legitimize questioned actions. For instance, Section 609 states, "Every consumer reporting agency shall, upon request and proper identification of any consumer, clearly and accurately disclose to the consumer: (3) The recipients of any consumer report on the consumer which it has furnished for (A) employment purposes within the two-year period preceding the request, and (B) for any other purpose within the six-month period preceding the request."

The inquiry process is the means by which credit bureaus choose to conform to the above section. By policy, the inquiry remains on the file for a period of two years. Through workshops and publications, credit bureaus have taught their customers (subscribers) to view too many inquiries as a danger sign. As a result, having more than two inquiries is often cause for application rejection on a point score system.

In the recent past, a rash of consumer complaints occurred when consumers charged that no specific authorization was given to generate an inquiry into their credit records; however, credit bureaus in most cases declined to remove the inquiries through the dispute process as described in Section 611 of the FCRA. Moreover, consumers who complained to the credit bureaus received form letters indicating their disputes would not be investigated.

An investigation by the Consumer Credit Commission showed that many of these consumers applied for a credit card with a major oil company, which generated an inquiry. The same oil company later generated a series of four additional inquiries to prevent the subsequent issuance of credit cards by competitors. Consumers who complained to the credit bureau were informed that inquiries must remain in their files for two years by law and nothing could be done to eliminate this requirement.

Section 605 of the FCRA states:

No consumer reporting agency may make any consumer report containing any of the following items of information:

1) Cases under Title 11 of the United States Code or under the Bankruptcy Act that, from the date of entry of the order for relief or the date of adjudication, as the case may be, antedate the report by more than 20 years.

2) Suits and judgments which, from date of entry, antedate the report by more than seven years or until the governing statute of limitations has expired, whichever is the longer period.

3) Paid tax liens which, from date of payment, antedate the report by more than seven years.

4) Accounts placed for collection or charged to profit and loss which antedate the report by more than seven years.

5) Records of arrest, indictment, or conviction of crime which, from date of disposition, release, or parole, antedate the report by more than seven years.

6) Any other adverse item of information which antedates the report by more than seven years.

Specifically, the law requires that "no" report shall be made containing any of the foregoing; however, credit bureaus repeatedly state to consumers that, according to the FCRA, negative information "must" be reported for seven years or, if it is bankruptcy related, 10 years.

Section 611 states:

If the completeness or accuracy of any item of information contained in his file is disputed by the consumer, and such dispute is directly conveyed to the consumer reporting agency by the consumer, the consumer reporting agency shall, within a reasonable period of time, reinvestigate and record the current status of that information unless it has reasonable grounds to believe that the dispute by the consumer is frivolous or irrelevant. If after such reinvestigation such information is found to be inaccurate or can no longer be verified, the consumer reporting agency shall promptly delete such information.

In recent years, TRW (now Experian), generated thousands of form letters and sent them to consumers who disputed information from their credit files. The letter informed these consumers that their disputes were determined to be "frivolous and irrelevant" and thus would not be reinvestigated.

The phrase "frivolous and irrelevant" is somewhat ambiguous and needs appropriate clarification. Certainly, the wording of a dispute could lead a credit bureau to believe it is frivolous and irrelevant. For instance, such a dispute might read, "I was 60 days delinquent in making a payment because I was in the hospital and could not make the payments." While this statement may be true and indeed unfortunate, the bureau considers it frivolous and irrelevant because it merely confirms the information on the report and does not challenge fact.

According to the Federal Trade Commission, disputes that *call for action* should not be considered frivolous and irrelevant. An example might be, "I was never late in making my payments; you have me confused with someone else. Please reinvestigate this matter."

Credit bureaus claim the majority of disputes received are deceptive. The legal "test" falls under the heading of "good faith belief." Good faith belief is determined through the use of the consumer's good memory and substantiating records.

The need for credit repair

Given the bureaucratic difficulties of dealing with the credit reporting agencies, it's easy to see how consumers quickly feel overwhelmed and are ready to pay credit repair agencies to take care of things. But the term "credit repair" is really a misnomer. No one can remove accurate and timely negative information from a credit report, except perhaps the creditor. Credit repair clinics prey upon those whose credit bureau reports contain negative information that interferes with their ability to obtain credit. And between bad debt and inaccurate credit bureau reports, credit repair has developed into a major industry abounding with scam artists. Most of the time, these agencies can't do anything you couldn't do for yourself—for free.

Credit clinic warning signs

According to the FTC, consumers should beware of credit repair companies that:

- Want you to pay for credit repair services before any services are provided.

- Do not tell you your legal rights, and what you can do for yourself for free.

- Recommend that you do not contact a credit bureau directly.

- Advise you to dispute all information in your credit report.

- Advise you to take actions that are illegal, such as creating a new credit identity.

The newly passed Credit Repair Organizations Act (see Appendix) is a federal law that makes most of these strategies illegal. However, it is too early to tell whether or not the law will be effective in stopping fraudulent practices by credit repair clinics, especially because nonprofit organizations are exempt from the regulations. (If a company can change its status to tax exempt, it may be able to stay in business.) It is best to acquaint yourself with the basic credit scams, because they're almost sure to reappear in a new guise, regardless of what the law says. The most basic scam takes advantage of the dispute procedure, and this scam is the least affected by the new law. Other common scams are covered in Chapter 6.

Taking advantage of the dispute procedure

The principal method employed by a vast majority of credit repair organizations to improve consumers' credit reports is the dispute procedure available to consumers under Section 611 of the FCRA. This section is designed to provide consumers with a self-help mechanism to correct credit reports that contain inaccurate or incomplete information. Correcting and updating such information benefits creditors as well as consumers by helping to ensure that credit-granting decisions are made on the basis of complete and accurate information reflecting the consumer's probable creditworthiness.

Many consumers who turn to credit repair firms for help have experienced significant credit problems in the past, which they hope to minimize. In the event that the negative information reported about them is accurate and verifiable, FCRA dispute procedures are unlikely to be of help.

Nonetheless, through advertisement and oral representations, credit repair organizations often lead consumers to believe that adverse information in their credit reports can be deleted or modified regardless of its accuracy. Their services are frequently sold on a money-back-guarantee basis, but consumers have reported difficulties in obtaining refunds. The company may be out of business, lack the funds to pay by the time consumers seek refunds or simply refuse to honor its guarantee. Credit repair organizations have caused economic injury to credit bureaus as well as to consumers in this regard.

The FCRA states that disputed information must be deleted if it meets any of three criteria: First, if it is inaccurate; second, *if it can no longer be verified*; and finally, if it is obsolete. So in addition to requiring that inaccurate information be removed, the law requires the deletion of disputed information that can no longer be verified or is found to be obsolete.

This is important to note, because experience has shown that some credit grantors do not verify information more than 25 months old. The reason for this is that the Equal Credit Opportunity Act requires creditors to maintain written documentation for a minimum of 25 months. Some time after that period, creditors purge the information. Thus, disputed information is, in fact, frequently deleted from the credit report because it truly can no longer be verified.

Credit bureaus are required by Section 611 of the FCRA to reinvestigate disputed information within a reasonable period of time and to delete information that they cannot verify. A credit bureau may delete accurate information from a consumer's credit bureau report because it is overwhelmed by disputes generated by credit repair organizations or because creditors fail to respond promptly to verification requests.

In the past, certain credit repair firms have attempted to deluge credit bureaus with numerous sequential disputes. They would send the identical dispute to the credit bureau six times—once every three days. The credit bureaus were not set up to handle such a strategy but attempted to do so using outdated procedures.

When a dispute was received, it would be given to one of 50 consumer relations clerks, who would in turn generate a consumer dispute verification form. The form was then submitted to the source of the information for a reply. Three days later an identical dispute would arrive, and the same process would be followed. The credit repair companies alleged that the disputes were not being returned to the credit bureau because the creditor (source) was confused. Perhaps he had returned one dispute form but not another, and as a result, the information was purged from the files.

The bureaus used two avenues to combat this situation. The first involved placing a coded message on the credit report, which, for a period of 30 calendar days, depicted the identification and relationship of the consumer with a particular consumer relations clerk, thereby avoiding subsequent frivolous or irrelevant disputes. Avenue number two involved the deletion of information that was not returned from the source within 20 working days; however, if it was later returned, it was added to the file and treated as new information. This procedure appears to have been effective in combating such strategies used by credit repair companies.

The development of the credit repair industry is a relatively recent phenomenon, fueled by the tremendous increase in the use of consumer credit over the last 30 years. The need for credit repair arose both because consumers found themselves in legitimate trouble, and because credit reporting agencies often mismanaged the information they sold to creditors.

The strategies employed by these clinics to remove legitimate information range from those I've just described—taking advantage of legal loopholes and bureaucratic inefficiency—to creating new credit identities and other questionable tactics. The credit bureaus have fought the clinics through state and federal legislative agencies. Laws have been passed regulating the practices of credit repair clinics in 35 states, and in 1996, the Credit Repair Organizations Act was passed at the federal level. The chapters that follow examine some of the more outrageous and dangerous scams that credit clinics have run, and provide an overview of laws governing credit repair practices.

Chapter 6

Credit Repair Scams

••

"Got bad credit? Bankruptcy, foreclosures, repossessions? No problem," declare newspaper and television ads promising to fix your credit record or get you credit cards and car loans. With millions of consumers struggling to overcome spotty credit histories, hundreds of companies have sprung up to take advantage of their predicament. Many of them, according to law enforcement agencies and the Better Business Bureau, are rip-offs.

Their "services" typically include blanket disputes of credit report items in hopes of having some or all of the negative items removed, or advising you or assisting you in creating a new credit file or identity. Sometimes they just want you to join the company, and be part of the multi-level marketing scheme.

Whether you hire such a firm, or decide to work for one, beware! The bottom line on credit repair, according to the non-profit National Foundation for Consumer Credit in Silver Spring, Md., is, again, that credit repair companies cannot (legally) do anything you cannot do yourself.

Under the Federal Fair Credit Reporting Act (FCRA), the credit bureaus must tell consumers what their credit files contain, if they ask. If the information is inaccurate, the consumer can challenge it free of charge. The credit bureau has 30 days to confirm the data or remove it from the file. But if legal judgments, bankruptcies or other pieces of your credit history are valid, nothing can change them. Still, consumers line up at the clinics, and they often get taken to the cleaners. A few examples of scams and typical experiences follow.

Take the case of Etta Grant, a Mineral Springs, N.C., hairdresser, who met with a Charlotte salesman for Nationwide Credit Corporation and agreed to pay $1,197 for services. She put $200 down and wrote six additional postdated checks (for $166.17 each) be cashed once a month.

Nationwide cashed three of the postdated checks, then deposited the fourth one early. There wasn't enough money in Grant's account yet to cover it, so her credit record actually got worse when it and other checks she had written bounced, according to the summary. The attorney general's office and Grant's private attorney were unable to get a refund from Nationwide. By 1994, the North Carolina Attorney General's Office was investigating 15 complaints against Nationwide Credit and two other companies at Nationwide's address.

According to the National Center for Financial Education, consumers nationwide and U.S. servicepersons overseas lost more than $50 million over a five-year period as a result of hiring fly-by-night operators to "fix" personal credit files, with little or no results. A typical scenario follows: XYZ Company comes into town and launches a major advertising campaign. They claim that they will remove everything from your credit report for $500. Within 30 days they have enrolled 1,000 people and skipped town—to the tune of a cool half-million. Not bad for a month's work and a little advertising.

Many such scams have been perpetrated by rings of proficient con artists. More often, however, the credit consultant begins with perfectly good intentions. What happens is usually something like this:

> *Bill Mooch spends his late nights watching cable TV shows about how to get into real estate with no money down or borrow millions of dollars on his*

credit cards. One night he sees a program about the dynamic opportunity in credit consulting. He calls the toll-free number, pays his $129, breezes through the course, and becomes a "professional credit consultant." Certificate and everything.

After that he sends in more money to become an associate. For only $1,000 more, he gets a briefcase and a set of business cards. Now he's really in business. He begins a massive advertising campaign. The credit cards are now at the limit. Then it happens. Money starts pouring in. He's got more business than he can handle. "Honey, what did you do with the Johnson file?"

Not to worry, though. He'll find the file later. Right now there are more important things to do—like sign up more clients. At $500 to $1,000 per client, Bill is on a serious roll.

Three months later the phone calls from the first clients start coming in: "I haven't heard anything on my case. My credit is still messed up! I want my money back."

Bill freaks out. "Honey, have you seen the Johnson file?" A week later, Bill and his wife decide to take a vacation—a permanent one. "What the heck, we can afford it," they decide.

In another instance, a credit consultant in Orange County, Calif., made a fortune by obtaining credit card applications from creditworthy individuals for a fee. Here's how it worked. The consultant would go to firms who wanted to get creditworthy individuals to accept their credit cards. He made deals with oil companies, department stores, banks, rent-a-car firms and many others, to pay so much for each valid credit application he turned in.

To put this on a wholesale plan where he could reap $20 or more per application, he went to the county records office and got the names and the mortgage holders of homeowners in the area. He called the homeowners, identifying himself as a representative of the mortgage holder on the property and stated that he needed a credit update. He would proceed to get all the information on a current application form and inquire as to which credit cards the people already held. All the companies he was representing whose credit cards the consumers didn't already have received these filled-out forms as applications for credit cards. He informed the homeowners that he had made arrangements with some companies to issue credit cards to them, that there was no obligation on their part to use them, but that they could come in handy in emergencies. Most people were amenable to this and raised no fuss. The consultant grossed more than $100,000 in a period of four weeks.

Changing your identity

Among the most notorious and dangerous of credit repair scams is the creation of a new credit file. In the past, the scam has worked like this: A credit repair company obtains a listing of recent bankruptcy filings from the public records. The company sends letters to the recent filers full of dire warnings about their inability to get any kind of credit, perhaps for as long as 10 years—no credit cards, car loans, personal loans or mortgages.

However, for a fee, the credit repair company promises to help by providing instructions on how to create a new credit identity. After paying the fee, the consumers receive instructions on applying for an Employer Identification Number (EIN) from the Internal Revenue Service. The credit repair company advises them to use the new employer ID in place of their Social Security numbers when applying for credit. It also advises them to use a new mailing address (usually that of a relative or friend).

Later, when a bank or department store runs a credit check on the alias, it turns up nothing, especially if the name has been changed. That is because the credit bureaus have no way of linking a fake ID with the real individual using it.

Credit One Services of Fort Bragg, Calif., is the largest such operation uncovered so far. Before being shut down in April 1992, with the arrest of its owner, John P. Ruggeri, and his wife, Nancy, Credit One had sold its $39 kits to 20,000 people.

In March 1992, the IRS put out an alert on Credit One Services, warning that anyone who got involved in the scheme could face tax fraud charges. The agency had noticed a rise in mismatched Social Security numbers that it could not explain. At the same time, the Better Business Bureau alerted the IRS to complaints about Credit One. The Los Angeles City Attorney's Office filed criminal charges, while the FTC, the State Department of Consumer Affairs and the Attorney General's Office filed civil lawsuits seeking fines. The U.S. Postal Service seized the Ruggeris' mail, and the FTC froze their bank accounts.

John and Nancy Ruggeri pleaded no contest to criminal violations of the state's credit repair laws and business code. Nancy Ruggeri was sentenced to 30 days in jail and 30 days under house arrest. John Ruggeri was sentenced to five months in the Los Angeles County jail.

The Federal Trade Commission has frequently warned consumers to be on the alert for unscrupulous credit repair companies that offer to create a new credit file by instructing individuals to obtain an EIN from the IRS. An EIN, which resembles a Social Security number, is used by businesses for reporting financial information to the IRS and the Social Security Administration. The bulletin states that these credit repair companies are instructing individuals with bad credit to use the

EINs in place of their Social Security numbers, along with a new mailing address.

The following are instructions from one such credit repair company on establishing a new credit identity:

> *To establish a new credit file, you apply with the Internal Revenue Service for a Taxpayer's Identification Number (also called an EIN). The required form is an SS-4 Form, which can be obtained by calling the IRS at 800-829-1040 and providing your mailing address. To avoid confusion, you need not explain to the IRS representative why you are requesting the form. (The form has many other uses, including being required for any new business.)*
>
> *Please follow the instructions listed below exactly.*
>
> *1. Print your name on Line 1.*
>
> *2. Go to Line 4a and print your current residence address.*
>
> *3. Print your city, state and zip code on Line 4b. Skip to Line 8a. Check the first box labeled "Individual" and write your Social Security number on the line to the right.*
>
> *4. Go to Line 9 and check the box labeled "Banking purpose" and write "loan" after the arrow to the right.*
>
> *5. Skip Lines 10 through 17c.*
>
> *6. Print your name in the area indicated at the bottom of the form.*
>
> *7. Sign and date the form where indicated.*

(If you currently have an EIN for business, you can still be issued another number for "banking and loan purposes." There is no need to complete the information on Line 17a, b, and c.)

You then return the form to the IRS by mail. The correct address for you to mail the form to is shown on the Instruction Sheet, which comes with the SS-4 Form. We do not recommend applying for your number by telephone as offered in the instructions. Instead, you should just mail your completed form to the IRS Center which services your area. In about three to four weeks, you should receive your Taxpayer's ID number by mail. This number is similar to a Social Security number for identification purposes and has the same number of digits, although you'll need to write it in the familiar three-digit, two-digit, four-digit format used in Social Security numbers.

After you have obtained your Taxpayer's ID number, you will then need to obtain a new mailing address for credit that is different from where you now live. Do not use any previous address you have used for credit in the past. Choose a friend or relative that lives in a different zip code, even if it's just one digit that's different. On any new credit applications, simply list this new address as your current residence address.

You will use your new address and Taxpayer's ID number on all credit applications you submit. You must never use your Social Security number or previous addresses on any credit application as this will cause your new credit file to become connected to your old credit file. It is, however, okay to list your current employer's name and address. This is usually required for any credit approval anyway and normally will not cause a connection with your old credit report.

Your Social Security number should be used on all Social Security documents; your new Taxpayer's ID number should be used on everything else, including your W2 form and for the payment of taxes. You can even have your employer change your records by completing a new W4 form with your new ID number. This will allow you to have paycheck stubs and income tax forms, which are sometimes required by creditors, that match your new Taxpayer's ID number.

It is also suggested that you change the address shown on your driver's license to your new address. This is for times when you are applying for credit and asked to show a photo ID, such as, when you are opening a new bank account. If your state requires that your license show your Social Security number, then try to obtain a new license with your new Taxpayer's ID number as well as your new address.

To establish a new credit file, simply apply for credit using your Taxpayer's ID number in place of your Social Security number and your new mailing address in place of your current address. Usually the creditor will have the credit bureau run a 'credit check' on you using the information you provide on your application. (We recommend that this first application for credit be a 'mail-in' type of application as opposed to a 'face-to-face interview' type of application.)

Normally, you will be declined for credit on this first application because of 'no credit history' or 'credit too new to rate.' However, by applying for credit with your new ID number and address, you literally 'force' the computers at the credit bureau into creating a new credit file, containing the new information from your application and showing only the one 'inquiry.' (This occurs due to the fact that their computer database search cannot bring up an existing credit file 'match.')

*In beginning your new credit, there are several things you must **not do:***

*1. **Do not** apply for credit at any bank, finance company or store that you have previously had credit with.*

*2. **Do not** open a new checking account at a bank that you have had any account with in the past.*

*3. **Do not** list any previous creditors that you have had an account with under your Social Security Number when filling out any new credit application.*

*4. **Do not** list any of your previous addresses on any new credit application.*

*5. **Do not** attempt to add favorable credit references from creditors that appear on your old credit reports."*

In a variation of this scam, the operator of a credit repair company in Los Angeles would assist his "clients" in establishing new credit files by transposing numbers of their Social Security numbers and changing their names and addresses. The clients would be instructed in how to obtain numerous credit cards with high credit limits. Working together, the operator and his clients would obtain large cash advances and make numerous credit purchases until all of the credit limits were exceeded. The clients would then file bankruptcy, wipe out the debts and reestablish credit under a new file. The scam would then be repeated over and over with various accomplices.

The law catches up

According to the IRS, people who change their Social Security numbers are cheating themselves of future Social Security payments for the years they work. Of more immediate concern, is that if your actions are determined to be fraudulent, you could be criminally liable for falsifying tax records. Credit repair companies that promote such schemes could be liable for participating in a conspiracy to defraud the government.

Here's what the FTC says: "It is a federal crime to make any false statements on a loan or credit application, which the credit repair company may advise you to do. It is a federal crime to misrepresent your Social Security number. It is also a federal crime to obtain an EIN from the IRS under false pretenses."

As if that weren't enough, the commission also warns that you could be charged with mail or wire fraud if you use the mail or telephone to apply for credit and provide false information. And you may be guilty of civil fraud under many state laws.

And, as of 1996, Congress passed a law that makes it *illegal* to advise consumers to alter his or her identification to hide accurate information in a credit report. Section 404 of the Credit Repair Organizations Act of 1996 states:

> *No person may (2) make any statement, or counsel or advise any consumer to make any statement, the intended effect of which is to alter the consumer's identification to prevent the display of the consumer's credit record, history or rating for the purpose of concealing adverse information that is accurate and not obsolete to any consumer reporting agency; any person who has extended credit to the person; or any person to whom the consumer has applied or is applying for an extension of credit.*

The Credit Repair Organizations Act also addresses other major problems with credit repair clinics; it prohibits clinics from accepting payment for services before they are performed, and requires the clinics to give you a statement explaining your credit reporting rights under state and federal law. For more complete information, see the Appendix.

In April of 1996 the FTC and 10 state Attorneys General launched "Operation Payback", a federal-state crackdown on fraudulent credit repair telemarketers. Included were specific actions against companies such as Giving You Credit and Partners in Vision International, Inc., of San Diego, Calif., and Clear Your Credit, Inc., of Chicago, Ill. Their multi-level marketing plan sold credit repair services through representatives who earned commissions on their sales and for recruiting new sales reps.

Among the tactics used by the defendants was to falsely claim that the FCRA *requires* deletion of an entire negative entry if it not 100 percent accurate. Other "Operation Payback" actions are pending in Illinois, Indiana, Massachusetts, Missouri, North Carolina, Ohio, Tennessee, Washington and Wisconsin.

Credit repair goes high-tech

The credit repair industry has been as quick as any to get onto the Internet to market their services. The package may look different in cyberspace, but the contents tend to be the same, and consumers should watch out. For example, in March of 1996, the FTC came to a settlement with two New York City law firms that were behind a deceptive advertisement posted on 3,000 Internet news groups.

In this case, the defendants posted an ad that stated, in part:

> *...Our LAW FIRM offers direct guaranteed effective credit restoration services by experienced attorneys...We have successfully facilitated the removal of Late Payments, Charge-Offs, Foreclosures, Repossessions, Collection Accounts, Loan Defaults, Tax Liens, Judgments and Bankruptcies from our clients' reports. WE GUARANTEE THAT YOUR CREDIT CAN BE RESTORED!*

The defendants charged a minimum of $500, with fees ranging from $125 to $700 for each item challenged.

The FTC charged that the defendants misrepresented their success rate for improving consumers' credit reports and misrepresented their ability to have derogatory information removed from credit reports regardless of the age or accuracy of the information.

Advance-fee loan scams

Sometimes the way our of debt may seem to be more debt. If you're thinking of taking out a loan to repay debt, beware of advertisements for "advance-fee" or "guaranteed" loans. The FTC is investigating complaints about companies that guarantee loans for financially strapped consumers and small business owners.

Advertisements that promise loans generally appear in the classified sections of local and national newspapers, magazines and tabloids. They also may appear in mailings, radio spots and on local cable channels. Often 900 numbers that result in charges on your phone bill or toll-free 800 numbers are featured in the ads. These companies also prefer to use delivery systems other than the U.S. Postal Service, such as overnight or courier services, to avoid detection and prosecution by postal authorities.

Some companies claim they can guarantee you a loan for a fee paid in advance. The fee may range from $100 to several hundred dollars. Small businesses have been charged as much as several thousand dollars as an advance fee for a loan.

Legitimate credit grantors may charge fees to process your loan application, but they will not guarantee that you will qualify for a loan. Illicit advance-fee loan schemes, on the other hand, either promise or strongly suggest that a loan will be provided in exchange for an up-front fee. Salespeople for such companies also may verbally promise that some or all of your advance fee will be refunded if your application is unsuccessful. Some fraudulent companies also may claim that your advance fee will be credited toward repayment of the loan. Usually none of these claims is true.

The FTC suggests taking the following precautions before responding to ads for advance-fee loans:

- Check out the company. Contact your local consumer protection agency and the state attorney general's office to learn if they have received any complaints about companies offering advance-fee loans.

   Keep in mind, however, that suspect companies often establish their operations in one state, advertise heavily for only a few months, collect their loan fees, only to close up shop and move on to another state before complaints are registered and local authorities have a chance to act. Therefore, just because your local consumer protection agency has no complaints on file does not mean that an advance-fee loan business is legitimate.

• Be wary of advertising claiming bad credit is not a problem in securing a loan. If money is not available to you through traditional lending institutions, it is unlikely to become available in response to a classified ad.

• Be cautious of lenders who use toll-free and 900 numbers. You may call a toll-free number which then directs you to dial a 900 number. You pay for 900-number calls, of course, and the charges may be high.

Be careful about making any loan agreements over the telephone. Do not give your credit card, checking account or Social Security numbers over the phone unless you are familiar with the company. This information can be used against you with other frauds. For example, if you give your checking account number over the phone to a stranger for "verification" or "computer purposes," the number may be used to debit (withdraw) money from your checking account.

Ask to review any company's offer in writing, and make sure you understand the terms of the agreement before you complete the transaction.

Obviously there are plenty of pitfalls in the credit repair business. Recent federal legislation has attempted to deal with fraudulent practices, but it remains to be seen if the new statutes will be effective in stopping the scam artists. One important loophole in the law is that nonprofit organizations are exempt from its requirements, and experience in California has shown that repair companies will apply for tax-exempt status, some by offering senior discounts or consumer education to qualify. In California, other companies either ignored the law, or went underground with their services by incorporating credit consulting into another type of business such as real estate, financial planning or auto brokering.

Acquaint yourself with the law, and you'll be prepared if and when the scam artist strikes. For a summary of laws affecting consumer credit information and repair services, see the Appendix.

Chapter 7

Questions and Answers About Credit Repair Companies

• •

Q: Are all credit repair companies ripoffs?

A: No. Some companies make an effort to help consumers correct mistakes on their credit reports and assist them in understanding credit reports. They also may provide assistance to people who are uncomfortable about contacting credit reporting agencies or negotiating with creditors.

However, many credit repair companies misrepresent what they can do by claiming to have the ability to remove all negative information from credit reports. Credit repair companies describe this process as "secret," but they don't do anything that you cannot do for yourself. Many credit repair firms have gone out of business after taking hundreds of dollars from individuals and doing nothing for them.

Q: How do credit repair companies "erase bad credit?"

A: The main way credit repair companies operate is that they bombard credit reporting agencies with requests to verify information. If a credit reporting agency cannot verify an entry, it will remove the information from the report. However, once the information is verified, it will go back in the report.

Q: What about companies that offer a guarantee?

A: Credit repair companies often claim they can "guarantee" to get you a credit card, regardless of your credit history. In fact, these companies do not always honor their guarantees.

In some cases, what you get is a "secured" bank credit card. (A secured credit card is a Visa or MasterCard that requires the cardholder to maintain a savings account equal to or double the credit line.) These cards often have high fees; it may cost you $100 to $200 just to get the card. In other cases, you get a card that only allows you to buy items in a catalog from a business that you probably never heard of.

Sometimes these credit repair firms will just take your money and run—you will not get any credit, regardless of what they promised.

Q: Isn't credit repair fraudulent?

A: Some companies try to get people credit by having them apply using personal financial information of people with good credit histories. It is a criminal act to apply for credit under someone else's name. Do not do business with one of these companies! You can, however, legally dispute inaccurate information on your credit reports, according to the Fair Credit Reporting Act.

Q: How can I find a legitimate credit service agency?

A: Before doing business with a company, contact the Better Business Bureau in your area and find out if there have been complaints about the company in the past. Also check with your local district attorney or consumer affairs office to see if the company is under investigation. If applicable in your state, ask the credit repair company to show you a copy of its bond and business license. If the company hesitates, take your business elsewhere.

The North American Consumer Alliance (NACA) is a non-profit consumer advocacy group that offers its members referrals to attorneys specializing in credit law. Call 800-497-NACA for more information. Other strategies, such as mortgage acceleration and rapid debt reduction are covered in my previous book, *Life After Debt*.

You may also be able to get free or low-cost help through Consumer Credit Counseling Service, a nonprofit organization with offices in most major cities in the U.S. This service assists consumers who have problems paying their bills (but are not yet in collection). They work out flexible payment plans to make debt repayment more feasible. Check your local phone directory or call 800-388-CCCS.

Q: What advice would you give to someone who is thinking about starting a credit repair company?

A: Start by reading everything you can find on the subject of consumer credit. Then get your own house in order first. Clean up your own bad credit before trying to help someone else. Then offer your services for free to a few selected friends and family members. Find out what it's really like to negotiate with creditors and deal with credit reporting agencies. If, after having done all that, you still want to become a credit consultant, check out all the laws in your area by contacting your state department of consumer affairs and your local district attorney's office. Obtain a business license, post the required bond and hang out your shingle. It is also important to make sure your contracts follow the guidelines of the law by including the required cancellation notices and other notifications as mentioned in this book.

Personally, I would suggest working under the umbrella of an attorney's office, a real estate broker or a nonprofit agency. This may exempt you from laws governing credit repair companies.

I would also suggest that you consider working as a consumer mediator under the Alternative Dispute Resolution legislation in your state. Or even better, start your own credit reporting agency. Contact Associated Credit Bureaus, Inc., 1090 Vermont Avenue NW, Suite 200, Washington, D.C. 20005-4905 for more information.

Q: What do I do if I have a complaint against a credit repair company?

A: Ask the company to return your money in full. If it refuses, write a letter threatening to sue the company in small claims court and report it to the Better Business Bureau, local district attorney's office, state attorney general, department of consumer affairs and the FTC. Keep a copy of all contracts and correspondence for your files, and send them to the appropriate agencies when you file your suit and formal complaints.

Chapter 8

The Importance of Good Credit

• •

A person with "good credit" manages credit well and pays bills on time. Good credit and a healthy credit rating are more important now than in past years. Here's why:

- Today you need good credit to get more credit. If you want to buy a house or a car, get a college loan for your child's education or simply apply for a credit card, the bank or credit union will check your credit report. An insurance company will check your report if you apply for more insurance.

- Good credit is convenient for consumers and businesses. In fact, many businesses strongly prefer the use of credit cards. For instance, it's very difficult to rent a car without a credit card. It's sometimes hard to rent a hotel room without one. Because of these policies, most people should probably consider obtaining at least one credit card. (If you do not handle credit well, however, you may not want to get one. A credit card is useful, but it may make matters worse for some people.)

- More and more employers are checking the credit ratings of prospective employees. Not all employers check, but those that do look unfavorably on a negative credit rating.

- Available credit is helpful for unplanned situations and emergencies: Having good credit does not mean being in debt! Rather, it means having the unused capacity to obtain credit. Credit capacity is useful for convenience, emergencies and unplanned bills. You may have a regular income and always pay your bills on time. Unfortunately, this *doesn't* equal a good credit rating.

Reasons for denial of credit

You may be denied credit because of "insufficient credit history." That may indicate you are just starting out in the world of credit. Perhaps you are very young, or you have experienced a major change in your life circumstances, such as death or divorce. Or it may simply mean that your lifetime of bill payments is not recorded in the computers that make up today's credit system. You may have paid your bills on a "cash basis," instead of with credit cards. Your credit may have been with local banks, credit unions and department stores that do not report monthly mortgage or loan payments to credit bureaus. So even though you've used credit all your life, you could apply for new credit and find that your credit report is blank. In any case, lack of credit history can hurt your application.

You may be denied credit because your credit report is mixed up with someone else's. Your personal credit history may be on your credit report and reflect positively, but your credit report may list the bad parts of someone else's credit history, too.

You may be denied credit simply because of your age, race or marital status. According to the Equal Credit Opportunity Act, it is illegal to discriminate on the basis of age, race or marital status, but it does sometimes happen. Many divorced and widowed women report special credit problems. When they were married, their credit was in their spouses' names, not their own. Their credit history is a blank.

Finally, some banks or other lenders may illegally discount nonsalary income. The Equal Credit Opportunity Act requires creditors who consider sources of income to consider Social Security, child support and alimony equally with employment income.

Causes of poor credit

If you're like most adult American consumers, you probably have at least one negative item on your credit report. In some cases, these negative items are inaccurate or misleading. Such inaccuracies can be caused by clerical errors, mistaken identities or fraud. In some cases you may find accounts that you believe to have been paid or current, reflecting an unpaid or delinquent status. In other cases, you may find accounts or other information that belong to someone else with a similar name. This is especially common with Juniors and Seniors in the same household.

Most of the time, however, the information found on your credit report will reflect your payment history for various accounts over the last several years. In light of the rising divorce rate, corporate "downsizing," economic recessions and problems with the health care insurance system, many individuals have found themselves unable to make ends meet at one time or another. Many of us have suffered medical problems, job layoffs or other temporary setbacks that caused us to fall behind on our bills for a period of time. Unfortunately such setbacks may continue to haunt us for years to come in the form of negative information on our credit reports.

Another major cause of poor credit is poor judgment. Many consumers overextend themselves with credit cards, signature loans, high car payments, second mortgages and overdraft checking privileges. Before they know it, they are over their heads in debt and unable to make all of their payments. In the most extreme cases, individuals have found themselves in bankruptcy court, small claims court or facing foreclosure. These "public record" items can be even more damaging to a credit rating.

Some of us are simply poor money managers. In spite of having more than enough income to cover monthly expenses, many individuals simply "forget" to pay all of their bills on time, or neglect to mail them before the due date. As a result their credit reports are littered with late payments, delinquencies and collection accounts.

Many people today are faced with personal financial problems. And things can look bleak when you're burdened with bills that add up to more than you earn each month. The reasons for financial problems are, of course, as various as the people who experience them. A loss or reduction in income. A change in marital status. Unexpected or emergency expenses. And then there's the ready availability of credit itself. Credit can be so convenient that it's tempting to use too much of it.

Whether it's the result of inaccurate information in your files or poor decisions in the past, a negative credit rating can cause you much hardship and humiliation. Remember, in any case, that you are not alone. More than 40 million American adults are rejected for credit each year.

If you are rejected for credit, you must take the necessary action toward repairing your credit. In the next chapters you will learn a simple approach to repairing your credit if inaccurately reported, or reestablishing your credit—regardless of your present situation.

Chapter 9

Seven Steps To Reestablishing Your Credit

• •

Your creditworthiness influences not only whether you can obtain a loan or purchase goods and services on credit, but may also affect employment, living accommodations or obtaining insurance. If you have a poor credit history, it will take time for you to regain your credibility with credit grantors. You must be able to show that in spite of previous debt problems, you can now handle credit in a financially responsible manner. To assist in this process, here are seven steps you can follow.

Step one: Pay off your debts

No matter how you got into credit trouble, it will help to restore your credit if you can bring your debt balance to zero. Lenders generally look more favorably on individuals who have solved debt problems than those who ignore them.

Begin by developing a liquidation plan to repay your debts. Make a list of all your debts so that you have a clear picture of your financial situation. Develop a repayment strategy; determine how much you can repay each month until you have paid off what you owe. Then, *pay your bills on time.* In my book, *Life Without Debt,* I explain the concept of a master repayment strategy in detail, offering insights into targeting which bills to repay first to get you out of debt with maximum efficiency.

Another excellent source of budgeting advice and assistance in developing a realistic repayment schedule is the Consumer Credit Counseling Service (CCCS). This nonprofit organization offers confidential counseling, assisting consumers with financial or debt management. (Bear in mind, however, that CCCS is largely funded by creditors, and it rarely recommends bankruptcy. Although bankruptcy is an extreme measure that should be avoided if possible, there are cases in which it is legitimate.) To find the office closest to you, call its referral number at 800-388-CCCS.

Another source of assistance is the North American Consumer Alliance. It can provide you with referrals to attorneys specializing in debt reorganization and negotiated settlement. This group has been highly successful in helping consumers avoid bankruptcy and settle accounts with the IRS and student loan administration. Call 800-497-NACA.

Step two:
Design a plan to manage your money

Often people develop financial problems because they overextend their credit use. In order to reduce the likelihood that you will find yourself in a credit crunch again and help you reduce debt, analyze your spending habits, create financial goals and set spending priorities. You have now begun to take control of your finances.

Step three:
Pay with cash

Even if you have credit available, you are more likely to change your spending habits by not using it. When you pay with cash or even a check, it forces you to recognize that the money you can spend is limited to the amount of funds you have in your checking account. Debit cards also serve this purpose since the amount you spend is immediately deducted from your account. You will need to make choices about what you can afford to buy and, therefore, you will have to determine your priorities. This sort of forced discipline should eventually enable you to better manage credit.

Step four:
Obtain your credit report

Most credit bureaus are part of one of the "Big Three" automated reporting systems: Experian, Equifax or Trans Union. After you have been denied credit because of negative information, you may obtain a free copy of your credit report from the bureau that supplied the information. The bureaus will allow you up to 60 days to make this request. Since each report is different, you should check your credit history in all three systems.

If you believe that there is an error in your file, you can write the credit bureau and fill out a dispute form. The bureau will verify the information with the creditor to insure that it is correct. If it is found to be an error, or if the information can no longer be verified, it should be removed from your report and the credit bureau is required by law to share the corrected information with the other bureaus. If the creditor states that the questioned item is accurate, and after you write the creditor there is still a disagreement, you may submit a written statement of less than 100 words explaining the dispute to the credit bureau, and it will become part of your record.

Step five:
Apply for secured credit

If you are trying to reestablish credit (or establish credit for the first time), one measure to consider is to obtain *secured credit*. Credit is secured when something of value is pledged to assure loan repayment, or if the responsibility for repayment is shared with a proven creditworthy individual.

One place to start to gain secured credit is access to credit cardholder privileges through your parents or spouse. You may also have a relative or friend who will co-sign a loan. Other options for reestablishing your credit reputation with secured credit include is providing an "enhanced down payment" for something (which might be as much as 50 percent of the purchase price of an item) or by opening an account with a utility in your name. If you do not have telephone, gas or electricity service in your name, you may try to open accounts with these companies. By providing a security deposit, you may be able to obtain this form of credit and establish on-time payment history.

If you have a savings account at a bank or credit union, you may be able to obtain a signature loan; that is, borrow a small amount using the savings account as collateral. Some banks will issue you a secured credit card. With a secured credit card, you will be required to put a deposit in the bank, in the form of a certificate of deposit or savings account. In exchange, you obtain a credit line, usually equal to one-and-a-half times the amount of your deposit. The deposit is frozen by the bank and acts as collateral from which the bank can draw if you do not pay on time, in effect, securing the card. However, remember that in addition, as with any credit application, you often will be required to have a minimum salary and minimum length of residence to be accepted for secured credit.

In the past couple of years, a number of major banks have launched secured cards. Interest rates on secured cards, which used to be 21 percent and higher, have fallen; some are now as low as their unsecured counterparts. Because of the attached deposit, the banks are assured of recovering their loans. As a result, some banks are now willing to offer secured cards to customers who have been through bankruptcy.

It is important to understand that secured cards are treated exactly like regular credit cards. For instance, businesses cannot tell that your account is secured by looking at the card or by phoning in for authorization. By the same token, if you fail to make payments on the card, you will be subject to a collection procedure. In other words, the bank will not simply deduct payments from your frozen collateral as they might with overdraft protection. The deposit will be seized as a last resort, only when you or the bank cancels the account and your bills remain unpaid.

Step six:
Apply for unsecured credit

A local department store may be more likely to issue you a charge card than a national creditor. If you can offer a reasonable explanation for your past credit behavior and show that you are now financially responsible, this information will generally help. Once you obtain a charge card and pay your bills promptly for a reasonable length of time, your credit line will probably be increased. If you cannot get a department store card, you may be able to begin by purchasing an item on the layaway plan. When you show that you are a reliable customer, the store will be more inclined to provide you with a charge card.

It is important, however, that you limit your credit applications to few stores, because each application will create a creditor inquiry that will likely appear on your credit report. Too many inquiries may cause creditors to think you are applying for more credit than you can afford and they may reject your application.

Step seven:
Continue to educate yourself

The credit system is extremely intricate and constantly changing. Every year, millions of Americans are caught up in a web of overwhelming debt and confusion. The rising level of personal debt, coupled with the introduction of dozens of new products in the credit marketplace, makes the need for timely, complete and user-friendly consumer education greater than ever.

Read as many books as you can find on the subject of consumer credit and personal finance. To save money, visit your local library. Your increased awareness of the system will help you to guard against repeating mistakes in the future. As you continue to educate yourself, you will also increase your confidence in your own ability to become master of your own financial destiny. Remember, debt is a form of slavery.

These simple steps, when diligently put into action, will dramatically improve your credit status—regardless of your present situation. The important thing is to begin now by putting these ideas into practice in your daily life.

For additional information or assistance, refer to the publications and resources listed in the back of this book.

Chapter 10

Repairing Your Credit Step-by-Step

•••

There's a brisk business among "credit repair" companies that charge from $50 to more than $1,000 to "fix" your credit report. In the past these outfits have taken money and done little or nothing to improve credit reports. Often they just vanished. Be wary of credit repair companies that "guarantee" to clean up your credit report. Such promises cannot be kept unless the information in your credit report is actually wrong or out of date.

Remember, too, that if there are genuine mistakes or outdated information in your report, you can fix them yourself. In fact, you can do anything a credit repair company can do—for free or for only a few dollars.

Disputing items on your credit report

The first step in repairing your credit is knowing exactly what your credit report says. If you have been denied credit within the past 60 days, you have the right to receive a free copy of your credit report from the bureau that provided negative information. However, I recommend a proactive approach; I believe every consumer should regularly (annually to every three years) review his or her credit reports from each of the Big Three bureaus: Experian, Equifax and Trans Union.

According to the Fair Credit Reporting Act (FCRA), you have the right to dispute any remark on your report that you "reasonably believe" to be inaccurate or incomplete. The act requires the credit bureau to reinvestigate those disputed items within "a reasonable period of time," interpreted by the Federal Trade Commission as 30 days. If the bureau finds that the information was incorrect, obsolete, or could no longer be verified, it must correct or delete the information.

How to dispute

1. Obtain a credit report and analyze the report for items you believe to be inaccurate, incomplete or obsolete. For example, you thought you owed $800 on your Visa card account. The account is presently under collection, but your credit report shows a balance of $900. This is inaccurate, and you have a right to dispute the entire account.

2. Send the bureau a dispute form (one should be enclosed with your credit report). If you don't have a consumer dispute form, follow the example at the end of this chapter. Be sure to include the items you are disputing, the names of the creditors (subscribers) and the account numbers. Indicate why you believe the item is being reported incorrectly. Examples: the amount owed is incorrect, the account is not yours, the account has been paid in full, the number of late payments is incorrect.

3. Keep track of the date the dispute was sent. If you do not receive a response within six weeks, immediately send a follow-up letter (see sample at the end of this chapter).

4. Obtain results of the credit bureau's reinvestigation. Most credit bureaus will notify you of the result of the investigation and send you a copy of your updated credit report.

5. Wait at least six weeks.

6. Repeat the cycle from step one another two to three times.

7. Keep a record of all correspondence. Make copies of all credit reports, disputes, replies and responses. If the reply is by telephone, note the date and the time of the call, the name of the person you spoke with and the nature of the conversation.

Chances are, once you dispute an item, you will receive a response within six weeks, but there have been many instances where bureaus have dragged their feet or lost track of disputes. If the bureau does not respond to your initial dispute within a "reasonable time," follow-up promptly. This time, insist that the bureau respond to your dispute immediately. Give them about four weeks to comply and be sure to maintain all copies of the correspondence.

If the bureau persists in violating your rights by refusing to reinvestigate your legitimate dispute, send them a final letter demanding action. This time, threaten to take legal action, and send copies of your letter, along with the original request, to the Federal Trade Commission and to your local office of the attorney general.

Sample statements of dispute

Under the Fair Credit Reporting Act you have the right to add to your credit report a statement of up to 100 words regarding any item(s) you wish to clarify. This statement will then appear on all subsequent reports sent to your credit grantors. Here are some examples:

- "This is not my account. I have never owed money to this creditor. Apparently, a mistake was made in the reporting."

- "On (date), I moved to another address. I notified all creditors, including (name of creditor) promptly. (Name of creditor) was slow in changing my address in its file. Subsequently, I did not receive my billing statement for (how long). Once I received the statement at my new address, I paid this creditor."

- "On (date), I was hospitalized at (facility). The medical bills were forwarded to my insurance company for payment. My insurance company delayed in paying and the hospital turned my account over for collection. Afterwards, my insurance company paid the hospital bill in full. The hospital's collection agency refused, however, to change the negative rating of my account."

- "This account belongs to my former spouse. My name is no longer on this account."

- "On (date), I ordered merchandise from (name of company) on my account. The merchandise was defective and I returned it to the sender. The company continued to send me a bill for the returned defective merchandise. The company went out of business before I was able to have my account properly credited."

Questions and answers about credit reports

Q: How will the credit bureau respond to my dispute?

A: The credit reporting agency may respond with one of the following answers:

- "We have changed your credit file as requested."
- "Your credit file will not be changed because..."
- "The party involved did not respond, so the information is being removed by reason of default."

Q: What if the response is no change to the report?

A: You have the right to request that the information be reinvestigated or you can place a 100-word statement of dispute in your report.

Q: How is bankruptcy reported to the credit bureaus?

A: Bankruptcy will show up on your credit report as a public record and may remain on your report for up to 10 years. Each account included in the bankruptcy will show up on your credit report as either "charge off" or "bankruptcy liquidation."

Q: Are there any positive items that can show up on a credit report?

A: Other than your identifying information, such as name, address, etc., the only positive remarks on a credit report will be for accounts that are either "paid satisfactorily" or "current account with no late payments." Nonrated items may include inquiries, accounts closed by consumer request or refinance. Other items on a credit report are usually negative, such as late payments, collection accounts, charge offs, tax liens, repossessions, foreclosure, etc.

Q: How can public record items be removed from a credit report?

A: If the item is incorrect, misleading or obsolete it can be disputed. If the bureau cannot verify the disputed information, it must be deleted from your credit report. If a lien or judgment has already been paid, but the report reflects it as being unpaid, you should contact the original creditor and request a discharge form. That discharge form is then submitted to the court clerk to be recorded, and a copy of the recorded document sent to the credit bureau as evidence that the lien or judgment has been satisfied.

Q: Do consumers have the right to ask that their accounts not be sent for collection?

A: Yes. If you are late in paying on your account, you should contact the creditor and ask to make an alternative payment plan. In some cases, you may be able to make reduced monthly payments or "skip" a payment without being penalized. In other cases (such as with an account that has already been charged off) you may be able to negotiate a settlement payment with the creditor.

Consumer statements

Under the Fair Credit Reporting Act, you have the right to add to your credit report a statement of up to 100 words regarding any item(s) you wish to clarify. This statement, or a version of it, will then appear on all subsequent reports sent to your credit grantors.

The consumer statement has often proven to be a very effective tool, especially if the amount of the negative account is small or if you have many positive items to cover a single negative. Here are some examples of consumer statements:

"Attention. Apparently someone has been using my identification to obtain credit. Please verify with me at (phone number) prior to the extension of new credit."

"Attention. This is not my account. I have never owed money to this creditor. Apparently, a mistake was made during reporting."

"During the period from (beginning date) to (ending date), I was laid off work without advance notice. I have always paid my creditors promptly and satisfactorily before and after that period. I am now gainfully employed and have been with the same employer since (starting date). "

Disputing with creditors

Another avenue to repairing credit is to deal directly with creditors that are reporting negative information about you to the credit bureaus. Creditors have the authority to change or delete items from your credit report. The first step in resolving such matters is to make sure that the reported item is correct and properly documented. If you believe the creditor delivered substandard service, sold you defective merchandise, misplaced your check, failed to deliver goods or otherwise did not perform its part of the agreement, you can dispute the item in the same way described for disputing with credit bureaus. A sample letter of dispute is included at the end of this chapter. It can be modified to fit your specific situation.

If the debt reported by the creditor is yours, you should attempt to satisfy it, at the same time negotiating to have the item removed from your credit report. You may offer from 70 percent to the full amount in repayment, in exchange for removing the negative item from your report. It is very important that the creditor's representative you work with has the power to authorize such an agreement, so do not hesitate to speak with a supervisor.

Negotiation strategies vary greatly depending upon the debt incurred and creditor you are dealing with (negotiating with a bank over loan repayment is quite different than negotiating with a department store over late payments). This subject is covered in detail in my book *Life After Debt*.

For more information

The FTC enforces several federal laws involving consumer credit. These include the Equal Credit Opportunity Act, the Fair Credit Billing Act and the Fair Debt Collection Practices Act. For single free copies of brochures about these laws or related publications entitled *Solving Credit Problems, Women and Credit Histories, Credit Billing Errors* or *How to Dispute Credit Report Errors*, write or phone: Public Reference, FTC, Washington, DC 20580; 202-326-2222. TDD: 202-326-2502.

Sample credit report request

Date
Name of Credit Bureau
Address of Credit Bureau
City, State ZIP

Please send me a copy of my credit report.

My full name is: (Jr./Sr./etc.)
My Social Security number is:
My date of birth is:
My address is:
Previous address (last five years):

I may have received credit in the last five years under the following names (e.g. maiden name, etc.):

Enclosed is a copy of a recent billing statement (or driver's license) as proof of my name and address.
(If applicable) I am making this request for a free credit report since I have been denied credit in the last 60 days based on one of your reports. A copy of the denial letter is attached for your information.
(If applicable) A check or money order for $8 is enclosed.*
Sincerely,

(your name)

*This fee pertains to credit reports if you have not been denied credit within the last 60 days. Some states mandate lower fees.

Sample letter of credit report dispute

Date
Name of agency
Attn.: Consumer Relations

Re: Your Name
ID#
Address
Telephone
Social Security number
Date of birth

     Please begin an investigation of the following items listed on my credit report that do not belong in my credit file.

Company's name	Account	Reason for dispute
_____	_____	_____
_____	_____	_____
_____	_____	_____
_____	_____	_____

     Please update my credit report and send me a copy at the conclusion of your investigation. Send the results to the following organizations that have reviewed my credit report in the past six months and/or to employers that have reviewed it during the past two years.

     Thank you for your help and prompt attention in this matter.

     Respectfully,

     (your name)

Sample follow-up letter to a credit report dispute

Date
Name of Credit Bureau
Address of Credit Bureau
City, State ZIP

Attn.: Consumer Relations Department

Dear:

On (date of first dispute), I sent you a request to investigate certain items on my credit report that I believed to be incorrect or inaccurate. As of today, six weeks have passed, and I have not yet received a response from you. Under the Fair Credit Reporting Act, you are required to respond "within a reasonable time." If the information cannot be verified, please delete it from my credit report. I would appreciate your immediate attention to this matter and your informing me of the result.

Yours sincerely,

(your name)
Address
Social Security number
Date of birth

Second follow-up letter to a credit report dispute

Date
Name of Credit Bureau
Address of Credit Bureau
City, State ZIP

Re: Your Name
Address
Social Security Number

To whom it may concern:

Four weeks ago I sent a follow-up letter stating that you had neither responded to nor investigated my disputes of certain incorrect items found on my credit report. Copies of that letter and the original dispute are enclosed.

You still have not complied with your obligation under the Fair Credit Reporting Act, which requires your company to ensure the correctness of reported information.

I demand that you immediately remove the disputed items from my credit file based on the fact that they are either inaccurate or unverifiable. I also expect you to send me an updated copy of my report immediately afterward.

If I do not receive your response within the next two weeks, I will file a complaint with the Federal Trade Commission and the state attorney general. In addition, I will not hesitate to retain my attorney to pursue my right to recover damages under the Fair Credit Reporting Act.

Please forward me the names and addresses of individuals you contacted to verify the information so I may follow up. Thank you for your immediate attention to this matter.

Sincerely yours,

(your name)

Sample dispute letter to a creditor

Date
Name of Creditor
Address of Creditor
City, State ZIP

Re: Your Name
Address
Account number

To whom it may concern:

I have recently obtained a credit report from (credit bureau). It shows the above account with your company was _____ days late (or it has been charged off, etc.). According to the best of my recollection, I have always paid this account promptly and satisfactorily. This incorrect information is highly injurious to my credit rating. I would appreciate it if you would verify this information and correct it with the above-named credit bureau immediately. If the information cannot be verified, please delete the account from my credit report.

Please inform me as to the result of your verification as soon as possible. Your immediate attention to this matter is greatly appreciated.

Sincerely yours,

(your name)

Chapter 11

The Ethics of Credit Improvement

•••

Since the publication of Life After Debt, *I have received hundreds of letters from consumers requesting information on the ethics of disputing accurate credit information. As I have clearly described in my previous books, there are certainly a number of legal ways in which accurate information can be removed from your credit reports. The question remains, is it ethical?*

The following article by Jayson Orvis is reprinted with permission from Inside Angle, the newsletter of the North American Consumer Alliance (NACA). I believe it addresses this important issue.

"Credit Repair" has not been kind to the American consumer. In fact, the phrase is synonymous with fraud. This is the stigma we face as we offer a membership wherein the client is offered an alternative to "credit prison." Because the nasty reputation of credit repair sometimes washes over into our space, we are often called upon to defend the ethics of our service.

Despite the disrepute which taints credit improvement, our service is clearly analogous to the service provided by defense attorneys. The credit report is no more than an allegation. Unfortunately most citizens never challenge that allegation. By enlisting the Law Offices through NACA to their defense, our clients employ us to enter a plea of "not guilty." We take an affirmative defense; we offer a reasonable alibi and leave it to the bureaus to substantiate their allegation. If the bureau claims to have investigated and affirmed the allegation, we appeal the decision. Eventually we find that most credit report allegations are at some point untenable and are removed.

Removing record of a negative credit account, which did actually exist, is undoubtedly ethically sound. We belong to a fundamentally capitalistic civilization and the credit bureaus capitalize on consumer information. Unlike our legal system, the bureaus take no oath to truth, equity and the common good. No American has the moral obligation to support any business venture or corporation, much less a corporation which may well destroy their financial life. The information tended by the credit bureaus is ethically "up for grabs."

The credit bureaus would maintain every piece of credit information forever if it weren't for federal law which has directed them to remove most items after seven years. In essence, the credit bureaus themselves practice credit repair, basically at the seven-year mark. If it is right to remove accurate credit accounts after seven years, why would it be wrong to do so in less time?

In relationship to the consumer, the credit bureaus do not concern themselves with the impact of the information. This information often misrepresents the creditworthiness of the consumer. By tagging good citizens as "deadbeats" the bureaus damage the creditors, the economy and, most importantly, the individual. Several policies and techniques employed by the credit bureaus appear most abusive to the American consumer; these we cite as justification of our opposition to the present credit reporting system.

Seven years (10 years for bankruptcy and some court accounts) credit bondage punishes the debtor unjustly. At no point have the credit bureaus ever conducted a study determining seven years to be the point of "deadbeat rejuvenation". The seven-year mark is entirely arbitrary. In fact, Dr. Bonnie Guiton, adviser to former President Bush on consumer affairs, remarked, "...it is our understanding that computer models that predict creditworthiness find most information that is more than two years old nonessential." Based on experience with our clientele, seven years is truly too long. Within a year or two most consumers completely recover from economic crises. For the remaining five or six years, they are left hobbled—forced to rent homes, pay outrageous interest on high-risk auto loans, forgo the convenience of credit cards and pay cash for every expenditure. By expelling the consumer from the credit loop, the economy suffers. Our clients come to us on the financial upswing. If they can afford our membership, they are most likely on the way back to financial abundance. These are consumers fully recovered from crises, reengaged to financial responsibility and anxious to re-enter the credit economy. For them we offer a deserved parole from the credit prison which they entered as their financial world fell apart.

The credit bureaus have not been able to maintain reasonable accuracy in their credit profiles. The bureaus claim an error ratio under one percent. In reality, studies conducted by neutral third parties have determined the credit report error ratio to be closer to 40 percent. Unfortunately for the consumer, the credit bureaus choose to err on the side of negative information. As our clients' files have passed through our offices, we have noticed a high incidence of file mergers—the worst kind of file error. In a file merger, the credit of another person with a similar name is spread onto the file of the innocent bystander. Oddly, the credit bureaus fiercely resist correction of these obvious errors. We have found the only way to prompt them to revision is through a lawsuit.

Credit reporting makes up only a small portion of the revenue which the bureaus claim each year. The databases really pay off in the sales of information. From generic target marketing lists to invasive personal investigative inquiries, the bureaus cull a pool of information larger than any in the civilized world. The end loser is the consumer who values his privacy. Horror stories keep coming about individuals whose jobs have been lost, insurance canceled, reputation ruined by sloppy collection and dissemination of personal information. This does not include the mass irritation experienced by consumers forced to wade through reams of junk mail. Privacy is a thing of the past—and the blame can be firmly placed on the credit bureaus.

America is not the only country in the world whose economy utilizes consumer credit. Other countries, such as Great Britain, extend credit based on the individual's present credit standing. A grand-scale revision of the credit reporting system in the United States would not throw our credit economy into chaos and distress. Until that day we should feel comfortable that the removal of negative credit accounts before the seven year mark isn't unpatriotic, it's not unfair and it's not unethical.

For more information, contact:

North American Consumer Alliance
6911 South 1300 East
Suite 500
Midvale, UT 84047
801-263-1373; 800-497-NACA

Conclusion

Where to Get Help

•••

The various consumer credit laws presented in this book are enforced by federal, state and local agencies. If you would like further information or have a particular problem you would like addressed, you can contact the appropriate agencies.

If your problem is with a credit repair company, credit bureau, debt collector, consumer finance company or retail department store, write to:

Division of Credit Practices
Federal Trade Commission
Washington, DC 20580

State and local consumer protection offices resolve individual consumer complaints, conduct informational and educational programs and enforce consumer protection and fraud laws. Local offices can be particularly helpful for both prepurchase information and complaint handling, because they are often familiar with local businesses and laws. Check your local telephone directory's white pages in the Government section for State Attorney General, Consumer Protection Division or Consumer Affairs Division. Your city attorney or district attorney office's fraud division may also be helpful.

Private organizations

The North American Consumer Alliance (NACA) is a non-profit consumer advocacy group that overcomes its members' tax, credit, debt and legal challenges through the engagement of professional legal counsel and the promotion of consumer awareness. Call 800-497-NACA or write:

North American Consumer Alliance
6911 South 1300 East
Suite 500
Midvale, UT 84047

The Better Business Bureau assists consumers by investigating disputes with companies and providing consumer mediation and arbitration services. Check your white pages under Better Business Bureau or write:

Council of Better Business Bureaus, Inc.
4200 Wilson Blvd.
Arlington, VA 22203

The Consumer Credit Counseling Service assists consumers who have problems in paying their bills (but are not yet in collection). Call 800-388-CCCS or write:

National Foundation for Consumer Credit, Inc.
8611 2nd Ave.
Suite 100
Silver Spring, MD 20910

Consumer Loan Advocates is a nonprofit organization that promotes consumer awareness and publishes *Rip-Off Reviews*, a monthly newsletter. Call 708-615-0024 or write:

Consumer Loan Advocates
655 Rockland Rd.
Suite 106
Lake Bluff, IL 60044

The National Center for Financial Education provides information about credit doctors and credit reporting agencies. Write:

NCFE
P.O. Box 3914
San Diego, CA 92163

Associated Credit Bureaus, Inc., a trade organization, offers a free brochure called "Consumers, Credit Bureaus and The Fair Credit Reporting Act." Write to:

Associated Credit Bureaus, Inc.
1090 Vermont Ave. NW
Suite 200
Washington, DC 20005-4905

Appendix

Summary of Federal Laws Governing Consumer Credit Reporting and Repair

....

Fair Credit Reporting Act

This act, effective since 1971, gives consumers the following rights:

- To know what credit information is held that relates to them, without charge, if they've been denied credit based on a credit report within 60 days.

- To have a reasonably accurate and complete file.

- To know who has received a report about them in the past six months and who has received a report for employment purposes within the past two years.

- To have information pertaining to them that they dispute reverified and corrected or removed if inaccurate or unverifiable. If there are changes in information reported, the credit bureau must send an updated report to credit grantors who have received a report about the consumer in the last year, or to employers who have received a report within the last two years.

- To place a statement in the credit reporting company's records if they continue to dispute the accuracy of an item after reverification.
- Not to have adverse information kept or reported for more than seven years, or up to 10 years for bankruptcies.

The 1996 update to the FCRA (effective October 1, 1997)

- Permits credit bureaus to supply information antedating the request by more than seven or 10 years if the consumer is applying for a loan or insurance of $150,000 or more, or if he or she is applying for a job paying more than $75,000 annually. (The qualifying amounts under the old law were $50,000 and $20,000 respectively).

- Requires employers seeking credit reports on current or prospective employees to obtain the employee's or applicant's written permission to receive the report. This permission must be signed separately.

- Stipulates that credit bureaus must share corrections to an individual consumer's record with other credit bureaus .

- Requires credit bureaus to establish reasonable procedures to prevent disputed information from being reinserted into files unless the supplier of the information certifies that it is correct. If information is reinserted into a credit file, the credit bureau must notify the consumer and give the name, address and phone of the information supplier.

- Requires creditors and other suppliers of information to promptly investigate and, if necessary, correct disputed information, whether it is brought to them by the consumer or the credit bureau. Corrections must be sent to all major credit bureaus to which the disputed information was reported.

- Requires credit bureaus to show consumers who request their reports the names of anyone or any business that has requested a credit report on the consumer in past year (or two years, if the inquiry was made by an employer).

- Limits charges for consumer credit reports to $8, adjusted annually for inflation. Some states have laws stipulating lower prices for residents.

- Requires credit bureaus to send reports free of charge, upon request, to consumers who have been turned down for credit within the past 60 days; to persons who are unemployed and intend to apply for employment within 60 days; persons who receive welfare payments; or persons who believe they are victims of credit fraud.

- Requires credit bureaus to provide toll-free numbers that consumers may call to block their files from pre-screening for credit offers. (This is called "opting-out.")

- Requires the bureaus to share requests received from consumers with each other.

- Requires bureaus to offer toll-free numbers consumers may call to ask questions when they are denied credit based on information contained in the report.

Credit Repair Organizations Act

The Credit Repair Organizations Act, enacted in 1996, was passed to ensure that prospective buyers of credit repair services are provided with information to make an informed decision regarding the purchase of such services and to protect the public from unfair or deceptive advertising or business practices. It prohibits the following:

- No person may make any statement, or counsel any consumer to make any statement, that is untrue or misleading with respect to the consumer's creditworthiness, credit standing or credit capacity, to any (a) consumer reporting agency, (b,i) person who has extended credit to the consumer or (b,ii) person to whom the consumer is applying for an extension of credit.

- No person may make any statement, or counsel or advise any consumer to make any statement, the intended effect of which is to alter the consumer's identification to prevent display of the consumer's credit record, history, or rating for the purpose of concealing adverse information that is accurate and not obsolete.

- No credit repair organization may charge or receive any money or other valuable consideration for the performance of any service which the credit repair organization has agreed to perform, until the service is fully performed.

- No credit repair organization may provide any services to any consumer until a written and dated contract for the purchase of services has been signed by the consumer. The contract must include, in writing, the terms and conditions of payment, including the total amount of all payments to be made by the consumer to the credit repair organization or to any other person. The contract must also give a full and detailed description of services to be performed including all guarantees of performance and an estimate of the date by which performance of services shall be complete or the length of time necessary to perform the services.

- Requires that the contract include the credit repair organization's name, principal business address and a conspicuous statement in bold face type that reads "You may cancel this contract without penalty or obligation at any time before midnight of the third business day after the date on which you signed the contract. See the attached notice of cancellation form for an explanation of this right."

- Requires credit repair organizations to provide consumers with the following written statement before any contract or agreement between the consumer and credit repair organization is executed. The statement must be separate from any written contract or other agreement, or any other written material provided to the consumer.

Consumer credit file rights under state and federal law

You have the right to dispute inaccurate information in your credit report by contacting the credit bureau directly. However, neither you nor any other credit repair company or credit repair organization has the right to have accurate, current and verifiable information removed from your credit report. The credit bureau must remove accurate, negative information from your report only if it is over seven years old. Bankruptcy information can be reported for 10 years.

You have the right to obtain a copy of your credit report from the credit bureau. You may be charged a reasonable fee. There is no fee, however, if you have been turned down for credit, employment, insurance or a rental dwelling because of information in your credit report within the preceding 60 days. The credit bureau must provide someone to help you interpret the information in your credit file. You are entitled to receive a free copy of your credit report if you are unemployed and intend to apply for employment in the next 60 days, if you are a recipient of public welfare assistance or if you have reason to believe there is inaccurate information in your credit report due to fraud.

You have the right to sue a credit repair organization that violates the Credit Repair Organizations Act. This law prohibits deceptive practices by credit repair organizations.

You have the right to cancel your contract with any credit repair organization for any reason within three business days from the date you signed it.

Credit bureaus are required to follow reasonable procedures to ensure that information they report is accurate. However, mistakes may occur.

You may, on your own, notify a credit bureau in writing that you dispute the accuracy of information in your credit file. The credit bureau must then reinvestigate and modify or remove inaccurate or incomplete information. The credit bureau may not charge any fee for this service. Any pertinent information and copies of all documents you have concerning any error should be given to the credit bureau.

If the credit bureau's reinvestigation does not resolve a dispute to your satisfaction, you may send a brief statement to the credit bureau, explaining why you think the record is inaccurate. The credit bureau must include a summary of your statement about disputed information with any report it issues about you.

The Federal Trade Commission regulates credit bureaus and credit repair organizations. For more information contact:

The Public Reference Branch
Federal Trade Commission
Washington, D.C. 20580

California Credit Services Act of 1984

In 1984, TRW (now Experian) successfully lobbied for a California law requiring credit service companies to adhere to a strict set of bonding requirements and regulatory restrictions. This law was known as the California Credit Services Act of 1984. Similar laws have been enacted in a majority of states, and the Credit Repair Organizations Act codified a number of the California Act's basic principles on a national level. Because the California Act is the prototype for so many state regulations as well as the federal law, we include an overview of it here.

The stated purposes of the act are to provide prospective clients of credit services organizations with the information necessary to make intelligent decisions regarding the purchase of those services and to protect the public from unfair or deceptive advertising and business practices. It defines a credit services organization as anyone who provides any of the following services:

1. Improving a buyer's credit record, history or rating.
2. Obtaining an extension of credit for a buyer.
3. Providing advice or assistance to a buyer regarding the above.

These regulations do not apply to:

• Regulated financial institutions (e.g., mortgage or loan companies).

- Banks and savings and loan associations whose accounts or deposits are eligible for federal deposit insurance.
- Licensed prorators (people who, for a fee, receive money from debtors and distribute the money in payment to the debtors' creditors).
- Real estate brokers licensed by the California Department of Real Estate.
- Attorneys.
- Brokers or dealers registered with the Securities and Exchange Commission or the Commodity Futures Trading Commission.

The credit services agency must provide the consumer with a written contract that contains the following:

- A complete description of the services to be performed.
- Any guarantees or promises about refunds.
- The date by which the services will be performed.
- The agency's name, principal business address and the name of a responsible representative of the agency.
- All terms and conditions of payment.
- A disclosure statement describing the consumer's right to cancel the contract within five days for any reason. The contract must be accompanied by a "Notice of Cancellation" form detailing the five-day cancellation rights and must contain a blank cancellation form.

The credit services agency must also provide the consumer with a written description containing the following:

- Information about the agency's trust account or bond.
- The approximate price that will be charged for a credit report.

- Complete information about the consumer's legal rights to review his or her credit record and to dispute the accuracy of items in the report.

If a consumer cancels the contract, the agency must return the deposit within 15 days of the date of cancellation.

Credit service agencies must also obtain a surety bond or establish a trust account of $5,000, or 5 percent of the total amount of fees charged during the previous 12 months (to a maximum of $25,000). If a credit services agency fails to provide the promised services, these funds will be used to reimburse the consumer.

It is illegal for an agency to charge money for referrals to retail sellers to which a person could apply directly for credit. Also, agencies may not make untrue or misleading statements to any credit reporting bureau or agency about an individual's credit standing or capacity, or advise an individual to make such statements.

Violation of any of these provisions is a misdemeanor, punishable under local and state laws. The agency is also vulnerable to lawsuits in small claims court or municipal court, depending upon the amount of monetary damages claimed. A consumer who files suit against a credit service agency can claim damages plus attorney's fees and costs.

In January 1993, the California Credit Services Act was amended to include the following provisions. Every credit services organization must:

1. File a registration application with, and receive a certificate of registration from, the attorney general's office before doing business in California.

2. Obtain a $100,000 surety bond from an admitted surety in favor of the State of California for the benefit of any person damaged by any violation of the Act (which must be maintained for two years after the credit services organization stops doing business in California).

3. Give the buyer, before the contract for services is signed, an information statement that contains: (a) a complete and detailed description of the services to be provided and the total cost or obligation to the buyer; (b) notice of the buyer's right to bring legal proceedings against the company's bond and the name and address of the surety which issued the bond; (c) a complete and accurate statement of availability of nonprofit credit counseling services; and (d) a statement of consumers' rights under the state and federal credit reporting laws to obtain their credit reports and to dispute inaccurate information in them.

4. Not provide any service to a buyer except pursuant to a written contract which includes a "Notice of Cancellation."

5. Complete the agreed services within 90 days of the date the buyer signs the contract for services.

6. Maintain an agent for service of process in this state (California).

Because the law exempts "nonprofit" corporations, many credit repair companies are applying to the IRS for tax-exempt status. Some are offering senior citizen discounts and consumer education in order to qualify.

Equal Credit Opportunity Act

Effective since 1975, this law was enacted to eliminate discrimination against women seeking to obtain credit. It was expanded to include the prohibition of denying credit based upon a person's race, color, place of national origin, religion, sex, age or marital status. It gives consumers the following rights:

- To be judged on an equal basis with all other credit applicants.
- To have joint accounts reported for both spouses separately after June 1977.
- To have income considered without regard to sex or marital status.
- To have regularly received child support and alimony payments counted as income, if requested.
- Not to be asked questions about birth control or childbearing plans.
- To obtain credit cards in their own names if they are married women.
- To know the reasons they have been denied credit.

Fair Credit Billing Act

This act, in effect since 1975, gives consumers the following rights:

- To file a written complaint with the credit grantor within 60 days of the bill they question being mailed to them.
- To receive an acknowledgment from that credit grantor within 30 days of filing the complaint and a settlement within 90 days.
- To forestall collection of the account until the dispute is resolved.
- To prohibit that credit grantor from reporting negative information regarding the disputed amount to the credit reporting agencies until the dispute process is completed.

Resources

Life After Debt
Career Press, Franklin Lakes, NJ, 800-CAREER-1
Not a rehash of old information, this book attacks the root causes of indebtedness and teachers consumers how to settle old accounts for pennies on the dollar. You'll learn how to stop collection agency harassment, billing errors and discrimination. Contains sample letters for reducing monthly payments, credit reporting disputes and negotiated settlements.

Life Without Debt
Career Press
This companion to *Life After Debt* provides advanced strategies for surviving in this credit-oriented society. It reveals inside information about the credit system, from credit cards to home financing, student loans to cosigning for family members. It also contains special sections for dealing with the IRS, auto financing, bankruptcy and the psychology of debt and spending. Learn to save thousands of dollars on mortgages, auto loans and credit cards.

Credit Secrets: How to Erase Bad Credit
Paladin Press, Boulder, CO, 800-392-2400

Contains a detailed description of the identification systems used by each of the major credit bureaus, along with dynamic strategies for circumventing the system and starting over with a new credit file. Also describes a method of "losing" your bankruptcy files and deleting any reference to filing for Chapter 7 or Chapter 13.

How to Beat the Credit Bureaus: The Insider's Guide to Consumer Credit
Paladin Press

Bob Hammond describes the deceptive web of information systems spun by the powerful corporate credit bureau syndicate and how it is used to victimize, humiliate and defile countless innocent consumers. More importantly, it will show you how to take legal action against an unfair system—and win. Includes documented successful lawsuits against major credit-reporting agencies.

Financial Dynamics: Volumes I-III

This is a three-volume home-study course. Volume I includes shocking new information concerning the coming cashless society, identification technology and electronic funds transfer systems. Volume II is a practical workbook containing sample letters, forms, resources and everything you need to delete negative information from credit files. Volume III describes 10 unique businesses that can be run from your home during your spare time.

Each volume may be ordered separately for $29.95 plus $5 shipping and handling (or all three volumes for $59.95 plus shipping and handling.) Send a check or money order to Bob Hammond, P.O. Box 51581, Riverside, CA 92517.

About the Author

Bob Hammond is one of the nation's leading authorities on consumer credit. He is the author of several books, including *Credit Secrets*, *The Credit Repair Rip-Off*, *How to Beat the Credit Bureaus*, *Life After Debt* and *Life Without Debt*. Hammond has been a guest on hundreds of radio and television talk shows throughout the country. In addition to conducting seminars and lectures on consumer credit and the coming cashless society, he trains real estate and finance industry professionals on how to help their clients get credit approval.

Hammond has been an arbitrator for the Better Business Bureau, an investigator for the Fair Housing Council and consultant to Consumer Credit Counseling Services of the Inland Empire. He also works with the North American Consumer Alliance (NACA), a nonprofit consumer advocacy group that helps consumers overcome tax, credit, debt and legal challenges through the engagement of professional legal counsel and the promotion of consumer awareness.

Hammond received his B.A. in psychology and sociology from the University of the State of New York, Regents College, and he studied screenwriting at the Hollywood Scriptwriting Institute.

Index

A

Advance-fee loans, 64ff
Associated Credit Bureaus
   (ABC), 21, 28, 105
Automated Consumer
   Dispute Verification
   (ACDV), 37-38

B

Bankruptcy, 89
Better Business Bureau
   (BBB), 22-23, 53, 104

C

California Credit Services
   Act of 1984, 113ff
CCN Group, 19
Changing identity, 56ff

Consumer Credit
   Commission, 44
Consumer Credit Counseling
   Service (CCCS), 23, 71,
   80, 104
Consumer Loan
   Advocates, 105
Consumer statement, 90-91
"Consumers, Credit Bureaus
   and The Fair Credit
   Reporting Act," 105
Credit Billing Errors, 92
Credit Data Corporation, 19
Credit improvement,
   ethics, 99ff
Credit repair agencies, 21-22
   changing identity, 56ff
   complaints, 72
   credibility, 69-71
   dispute procedure, 48ff

"erasing" bad credit, 69
guarantees, 70
Internet, 63-64
scams, 53ff
starting your own, 71-72
warning signs, 47-48
Credit Repair Organizations
Act, 48, 51, 62-63, 110-111
Credit Repair Rip-Off,
The, 121
Credit reporting services
advance-fee loans, 64ff
Equifax, 15, 20-21, 27, 31,
37, 42, 81
Experian, 19ff, 27, 31,
37, 42, 46, 81, 113
five "Cs," 43
industry secrecy, 43
mentality, 42
Trans Union, 20-21, 27, 31,
37, 42, 81
Credit reports
consumer statement, 90-91
contents, 25-26, 28ff
credit scoring, 30ff, 38-39
disputes, 85ff, 94ff
negative notations, 29-30
neutral notations, 29
positive notations, 29
public record items, 90
requesting, 27, 93
"risk score," 32, 38-39
Credit rights, 111-113
Credit scoring, 30-32, 38-39
Credit Secrets, 121

D

Debt Counselors of
America, 24
Denial of credit, 74-75
Disputes, 85ff, 91-92, 94ff
Division of Credit
Practices, 103
Dobbs, Samuel C., 22

E

Educating yourself, 84
Employer Identification
Number (EIN), 56ff
Equal Credit Opportunity
Act, 92, 116-117
Equifax, 15, 20-21, 27, 31,
37, 42, 81
Experian, 14, 19ff, 27, 31,
37, 42, 46, 81, 113

F

Fair Credit Billing
Act, 92, 117
Fair Credit Reporting Act
(FCRA), 14, 19, 27, 32,
33ff, 42ff, 48f, 53,
85, 88, 90, 107ff
Automated Consumer
Dispute Verification
(ACDV), 37-38
incorrect information, 36
limitations on access
to information, 33-34

reviewing your file, 34
time limits on adverse
data, 34ff
your own statement, 36f
Fair Debt Collection
Practices Act, 92
Fannie Mae, 38
Federal Trade Commission
(FTC), 15, 38-39, 46-47, 62,
64-65, 86-87, 92, 113
FileOne, 19-20
Financial Dynamics:
Volumes I-III, 120
Freddie Mac, 38

G

Good credit, 73ff
Great Universal Stores
PLC, 19

H

How to Beat the Credit
Bureaus: The Insider's
Guide to Consumer
Credit, 14, 120
How to Dispute Credit
Report Errors, 92

I

Inside Angle, 99
Internal Revenue
Service, 56-57, 62

L

Life After Debt, 71, 92, 99,
119, 121
Life Without Debt, 80, 119, 121

M

Michigan Merchants Credit
Association, 19
Money management, 80

N

National Center for Financial
Education (NCFE), 105
National Foundation for
Consumer Credit
(NFCC), 23, 53
Negative notations, 29-30
Neutral notations, 29
North American Consumer
Alliance (NACA), 71, 78,
99, 102, 104

O

ONE-PAY, 24
"Operation Payback," 63

P

Paying off debts, 79-80
Permissible purpose, 19
Poor credit, 75ff
Positive notations, 29, 89

R

Reestablishing credit, 79-84
  credit reports, 81-82
  money management, 80
  paying off debts, 79-80
  secured credit, 82-83
  unsecured credit, 83-84
Rip-Off Reviews, 105
"Risk score," 32, 38-39

S

Secured credit, 82-83
Secured credit card, 70

Social Security, 57
Solving Credit Problems, 92

T

Trans Union, 20f, 27, 31, 37, 42, 81
TRW Information Services, 14-15, 19, 27, 42, 46, 113

U, W

Unsecured credit, 83-84
Women and Credit Histories, 92